Table
Talk

How to Decide & Deploy Creativity in Life, Business and Career.

OKETA, Daniel

GIFT this BOOK to SOMEONE

SPECIAL

From

....

To

....

Date

....

Occasion

....

Table Talk

How to Decide & Deploy Creativity in Life, Business and Career

BY

OKETA, Daniel

Copyright

Table Talk: How Decide & Deploy Creativity in Life, Business and Career.

Disclaimer:

The Ideas herein are based on personal researches and successful approaches used. Therefore the author and publisher is/are free from any result it generates for the user.

For Information and Address

OKETA, Daniel
Abuja, Nigeria.
Call +234-703-738-4814
Oketadaniels@yahoo.com

Contents

Preface

This book is divided into two parts. Part one has the concept of creativity and some creativity approaches to business and life endeavors. The Secord part deals more on maintaining and sustaining success in business career and life in general.

This book is carefully packaged as a result of great yearning for a three way success in life, career and business. It brings people's creativity in focus and fuels entrepreneurship spirit and development. It doesn't matter if you are a public servant, business leader, SMEs, and private individuals of any size, form or colour; you will find this book effectively useful.

It is desired for both the inner and outer transformation of a person, people, community or nation. This why you are not limited to ideas encapsulate here but it serves as a guide and lead to discover the best ways to apply yourself to diverse solutions and techniques for success.

PART ONE:
Creative Entrepreneurial and Business Strategies

Series One: Introductory Expert One

If the world does not come to an end in the next 30 minutes then the information in your hand will help you a great deal; whoever you are now or want to be.

We are going deep and passionate with creativity to open us to our desired future or vision. Until we begin to think and act creatively, we can hardly create or discover anything or know how best we can be. This is why we identified and listed some creative innovative approaches that can help people across the globe to identify and release their potentials for greatness and efficiency. We believe this world is always looking for someone who can take a bold step that everyone can give way but still render support and help in innovative or creative entrepreneurship. Some of the questions that will be answered creatively and inwardly here are:

- *What do I need to know to get to where I should be?*
- *What do I need to do where I am now to get what I need?*

Someone told me that according to the law of words, man is not designed to say what he has but to have what he says; therefore, I will add that man is designed to use what has, because every man has something. For instance, it is saddening when people are looking for a job while they can create multiple of jobs for themselves and even for others and get highly rewarded. We believe that what you know will determine your position or where you will be and your position determines greatly what you will do and your reward.

Series One: Harnessing Your Creativity for the Future

Creativity or innovation is not necessarily creating or inventing a new thing, but discovering the power or force behind a thing. That is the power or force to lift something or pull another down. All things have already been created by God, we can only discover how to use and benefit from them; and more so, that solutions to our challenges are always around us. Therefore, we can find a new use to everything, or find a new approach to an old issue.

Creatively makes you stand out tall even though you are small in stature; you know why, you are soon going to stand in front and in the podium. It exposes your excellence and excellence is the cure to any form of prejudice or discrimination.

Creativity is a matter of choice and not to be compelled on anyone. If you are not creative, you are simply destructive. You cannot stay on the fence or middle ground because even if you stay on the fence; you are not safe, because you may soon fall. But in case you have fallen, it is time to get up. Innovation and creativity has found a place and importance in business, relationship and personal life.

How to Build Your Creativity

1. **Have an open mind:** Nothing enters a closed mind. A close mind is too knowledgeable to be taught or to learn from anyone; a close mind is someone who is frustrated and hopeless. The First key to innovation is an Open mind or will; a desire to learn or know more always. An open mind means deciding to be creative. For example, deciding to read this piece is a matter of Open mind.....let this sink. Most people don't care what others have known 'they always know it all'. Such kind of persons may never become creative and even if they do, they won't go for the application techniques for transmission and success. Never stay in one day without desiring to learn and writing down something you have learnt or discovered; business, career or otherwise. Unless

your intentions and plans are evil, you should write them down. People who do evil don't write it for fear of been seen or caught.

2. **Leverage.** The word leverage means influence, power, or weight describing the act of relying or making use of the availability of something to move forward or grow. This is to take advantage of where you have power- where you are, what you are, what you already know or the people you know. I spoke to someone that; where she is now could be for her most benefit since she can't change it at that point and therefore she must use it because tomorrow she might not be there anymore. Leverage on the fact that there is a problem on ground in your country or state or region of community or school or work place so you can make or show something good and better. Everybody any everywhere are just unique in a way, just leverage on their goodness or worst case to succeed. Leveraging helps you to build on your

most area of excitement or expertise occasioned by a universal force. More so, you can simply learn a new thing. Leverage on your success by teaching others how to come out of their problems; remember you had that challenge before-how did you overcome it? For example, once I wrote a few titles, I appealed to and distributed them to my associates and friends to help me edict- that is leverage because I could have paid for the same service. Although they may be rewarded by me; it will be at a time that keeps me out of pressure.

3. **Put your thoughts and Imaginations to action**. Your thoughts are a reflection of what is possible or you can do. If your thoughts are right (benefit to you, to others or no harm to anyone), go ahead and act towards it even if the actions is very small at that time. The fact is, do as much (not less) you can do per time. If your thought is evil, kill it by changing focus or location. Never under-rate or

underestimate your thoughts or the power of your thoughts, it is the beginning of all things.

4. **Apply New Techniques**: Don't be rigid to new or unconventional ways of doing things especially to accomplishing task. Too much conventionalism is the trap of the devil and tradition. Applying new techniques also mean doing something which might not be new but is new to where you are applying it. This can be achieved my learning what others have done elsewhere and yet not completely relying on their style.

5. **Add Value/New Uses:** Also find new uses to things that you are not using or lying in waste; give them out or sell them out for auction. Let nothing lay desolate around you. If you are not using your car, even if you bought it for $1m, go ahead and give it out for $200,000 if that's the fee that is offered. Convert the money to another profitable thing. But never sell a Land to use the money to trade cars.

Sell the land to buy another land with a profit or high value. There is another way of adding value to existing things; that is exploring more uses of a thing, taking advantage or adding more flavour to meet up with technology and/or development. For instance, if your land is not in use for the building project or purpose now; you can start a farm on it or rent it out.

6. **Help and Honour:** No matter whom you are or what you are, if we all live to help someone or others achieve their goal or solve their challenges then we can receive help or means to attend to ours as well. We are needed because we can help. That is why no matter how small you think some has helped you; they deserve a reward. We live in a world where most people are yet to learn the path of honour; in honouring people and receiving honour. Honour is a deserved gift we give or received for a help and difference in our lives, careers and business. The path of honour gives us

an opportunity to be recognized and honoured for our difference even through the honour we bestowed on others for their difference of a connection or relationship. When you think creatively, you are bound to honour the smallest creativity or support you receive and in such form you create the path of your honour.

7. **Dressing:** A lot of people don't know that dressing is creativity. Your dress creatively speaks before you speak. Dressing well and good without 'offense' to those that look upon you is also very creative and powerful. I need not overemphasize this. If you are a baby in your dressing (dressing as if you are too innocent to know that people value and respect dressing), you will bag a baby address with less concern. A womanly dressed lady, get a womanly respected address. Your ability to dress without offense make people to stay with you, listen to you and receive your creative input for your own distinction and difference.

8. **Work or Walk with Someone:** It is creative and powerful to identify a like-mind. The power of two is greater: Information or idea is shared faster, confidence is built and strength is supported easily. If any idea has supports and commitments from like minds, it has the capacity to fly; that is the force to take off, maintain altitude and move forward to the desire destination.

9. **Get the owner of Creativity Involved:** There is someone that created the Universe because nothing ever exists of its own. You can exist in your class but not alone. Relying on God by purposely seeking to understand Him as much as you can gives you wide access to become greatly creative and successful and to help you apply all the other forms of creatively listed.

10. **Have a Plan:** It is very creative to have a plan or write your instruction and thoughts down. Your

thoughts and imagination mean less if they cannot be structure out as a plan.

Creativity/innovation is a sure means with an amazing result that can launch us into stardom, fame and prosperity. As you go out from today onward ...remember it is all about creative thought and actions. It's time to start being very creative in all things. Always ask within you like this: HOW CAN I BE CREATIVE ABOUT THIS THING AND ACHIEVE RESULT QUICKLY OR TIMELY? Remember, those who don't learn a new thing cannot be creative, because they are the same always. Creativity works with change and solution mindedness. A change is not a problem but an opportunity to excel; much so that a challenge is not a wall but a door for promotion.

Summary: What did you think you learnt: what point struck you from the piece or in your heart: please use pencil

....

....

....

....

....

....

Series Two: Entrepreneurship, the Graduates and Non-Graduates Gap

The core and stand out of entrepreneurship is the ability of any one to be creative and bring out something where it seems impossible or difficult to solve a challenge, manage resources and make profit. We have noticed a dangerous pattern and precedents in most parts or countries of the world in business, employment and the supposed education gap between Graduates and Non-Graduates. This is in the fact that non-graduates are all in business, fairing and leaving better lives than most graduates. The following reasons have been identified:

1. A graduate wants to get everything secured before living

2. Feels they cannot start a business from scratch

3. Always need or High investment and business start-up goals and capital

4. They want to be employed in the best reputable companies or organizations

5. They want to work for government and in government agencies

6. Some often pile up certificates for the sake of owning them.

7. Does not have a concrete well structured investment plan.

8. They always seem greedy and too exposed to support themselves in partnerships.

Non graduates make a living faster because they invest and start a business no matter how small it seems and they soon explodes in profit; they are also willing to come together easily even as couples and partners to start up. But for graduates, they wait looking for job and become redundant, outdated and outmoded because no company want to put people on the job without a requisite training, experience or a unique idea for profit proposition. Also in some cases, they end up more idea-less or less creative even if they have gained employment; because they show antipathy towards personal development; reading and mentorship.

In most cases, parents and/or guidance of graduates are ready or willing to spend huge amounts on their loves ones by offering to buy them jobs in many ways claiming that such jobs has pension or gratuity or security. They only need to understand that the security of any job is one's ability to perform and deploy solutions. That same money for buying jobs and indulging in all forms of needless sharp practices could be used to support and test them in business and setting them up in entrepreneurship. Other graduates or even non-graduates result to criminality and most times cry out the fool that it was because they could not find a job on the surface of the earth. This situation puts more weight on government for recurrent expenditure; salary over heads, pension and allowances in instead of concentration on infrastructural development and provision of social and basic amenities for healthy private sector, business competition and entrepreneurship.

The World's Leading Secrets

One success techniques employed by world leading economies and even those that have transformed from 3rd world to first world countries are greatly rooted in entrepreneurship zeal. The power of every entrepreneur is to start small with a unique or great idea;

it provides an edge of experience in management and business marketing techniques for more successes and brand ownership. Even God I can boldly say is an entrepreneur who started small with one man and a woman and now has all of us in the entire world; that is having a very mighty idea with a small beginning. We ourselves began small as a baby. This is to say the world started with entrepreneurship and can be sustained still by it today.

The Spirit of Entrepreneurship

Entrepreneurship is a spirit, a character rather than a concept. It is the particular idea of meeting needs or uniqueness that can be called a concept. Entrepreneurship is an inner awareness of success driven life that is marched with the needed action at all points.

One of the greatest ways to start off in your unique entrepreneurship pursuit and success is to begin to think as an employer even from the college or university. A thought is not a mere wish; everyone thinks and wishes for the best, yet very many end up poor, weak and frustrated. A thought is a plan not just a wish if you want to really succeed; it is well written down and developed upon daily over a long time. By this, the planner is setting up and positioning his/her for investment opportunities and openings.

Summary: What did you agree with?

....
....
....
....
....
....
....
....
....
....
....
....

Series Three: How to Get a New Job or Change Your Job

If you say 'I want a pay job or employment'- what I expect next to hear from you is 'I need an opportunity to release my potential and cross bridge ideas and contact'. I believe that after the realization of your potentials and proper job propositions as illustrated here, you will have what you want. In here are six (6) level discoveries with a practical section of how to work anywhere or with anyone and release your best immediately to achieve your desires. No matter how old or young you are, these discoveries will help you.

1.   Discover now that you already have a Job as well as potentials

2.   Offer Freelance in Passion or Core Knowledge

3.   Be Very creative in your dealings

4.   Do the Practical

5.   Interview Wisdom

6.   Leave Fear alone

1. Discover now that you already have a Job as well as Potentials

a. I have Potential(s)

What potentials do you have? Your potentials may not be how energetic or physically strong you are but greatly depends on the information you have and how to use it effectively for profit. One way to receive or acquire information is determined by the problem you are seeking to solve or can solve. The problem you can solve (solution you have) determines how payable or rewarded you can be. There is no one on the earth who does not have potentials and who cannot have or develop some potential.

This means that **P=I=S=M**

Where **P**=potentials, **I**=Information, **S** =(solutions to problems) and **M**=Money.

Don't ever forget **P.I.S.M** to summarize the fact that a problem is a seed for money or reward. The problem you can identify and/or solve represents the potentials you have or build upon. Pick up a note and write down 1-3 things you can do or know. You will learn how to add creativity to it later. For example, if you simply know that some things cost less somewhere and sold higher in another place, it is potential information for success. Everyone knows something that others don't know or that others will need. Also everyone have something that others may need, the difference is how to creativity bring them out or use those information or skills as potentials to trade with.

Be eager to reward and appreciate others for their difference: Let us go back to how the world started; pure entrepreneurship which is to give me what you have and I give you what I have. Show me what you know and I give you what I have.

b. You Are Not Jobless

I believe you are not jobless. How? You have a job right now no matter where and who you are. First, your job may be to find a job or better still create one or two or three. Secondly, your job is how to be creative in your currently location or employment for more relevance, reward and growth. You see, I am not just giving you a hope, am telling you how things work so it can work for you. Therefore, are you jobless?

My Job Right Now

Do you know my job right now? I am building and developing your potentials on the inside for your outer usage. I am teaching, coaching, and training you on efficiency for your personal and career growth and explosion. This is like a Life Support System (LSS) and I believe you are in the Intensive Care Unit (ICU) right now. You must be on your feet so you can walk and run, immediately you finish eating this book. This is my expectation and this is my plan.

c. Try to figure out solutions

What do you know, what can you do. If someone asked you, what can you do for our organization? Or to say, this is the project we are running or thinking of running (they may not tell you this), because they may not have thought of it yet but you need to figure out in order to create your own relevance based on what they need. If I will figure out your challenge no matter how little, then you would call me for a bigger one sometime very soon. You know what, problems and challenges are coming up every minute, and every day.

You need to figure out needs: you see, if I were to be walking on the road and you approached me, called my three names or even two, and told me a few things you know is my problem and gave me an offer to help me solve them. Don't you think I will listen to you and probably get you a deal? That is it. Be specifically moved by the problem of those around you and find a way to solve it. Get involved.

The Clue: Problem solvers don't talk about the problem once they know it, they find and talk solutions. Problem solvers don't say 'something has to be done about this', they say something like 'we or I have to do something about this' 'can you give me some time to think about this?' 'We will need such and such things to handle this matter'. Problem solvers are thinkers, planners and researchers.

Look around your community, work-place, school etc and be attentive or sensitive to identify problems. Then look for the solutions and offer them.

2. Offer Freelance in Passion or Core Knowledge

Freelance means offering your service without being paid at all or being less paid. Passion leads someone to freelance; work even without the appropriate wage or reward but anticipation of realizing vision or goal. It can also be said to be volunteering and sometimes based on what you know or have learnt. It is a form of penetration for a deeper run or release of potentials. It is a perfect way to start; learn or contribute, gain experience and even to be rewarded.

Once I was up; I saw an ICT and Entrepreneurship company and I walk right inside and demanded to see the manger or head of training. I met him and offered to give an extra hand but *FREELANCE* lecture in ICT and Computer Basics. He agreed and took me in; and I was not to come every day but only when I have some classes.

Now here is the deal, at first I did not offer to be paid but the man in charge said, they will have to pay me but not in full. I agreed quickly; "it's ok, it is not a challenge" and a deal came up and I remembered I was not to transport to that office at that time. You see even though I was not paid as much as I would have expected as a full time worker which I was not, I got my share and built a relationship. They saw that I was good and efficient. That same organization has called me up twice as a Resource Person for some training in and out of town; which I would be paid this time not as freelancer but a professional. I still have that relationship should they be another deal.

The Clue: Offer to serve first. The fee or reward will surely come because it is a divine debt being sowed. But if you are given the opportunity; ask for or receive your reward.

3. Be Very creative in your Dealings:

We can all be creative in some ways without hindering each other's progress. Keep in mind the seven points discussed in the beginning chapter about harnessing the

power of our creativity to better our future as

1. Have an open mind

2. Leveraging in what we have, or where we are.

3. Put your thoughts and Imaginations to action.

4. Applying New Techniques

5. Adding Value/New Uses:

6. Determining your Dressing and

7. Working or Walking with Someone

8. Help and Honour others

9. Involve the Creator

10. Have a plan well written

4. Practical Section:

1. Pick your pen and note identify where you need to work to release your potentials and get rewarded:

   I. Identify any company or organization far or around you that you like to work with not work for

   II. Go do a research about the Company- you can use their website

III. Find a lope hole or problem they have that you can solve innovatively or that you can talk about. Offer proposition that could contribute to their growth. Identify where you can strengthen that organization.

IV. Show up in their office and demand to see the head.

    a. *"I want to see the manager or CEO or head, something of that nature: Why? Who are you and where are you coming from? Give them the answers politely; James Dyakona, I have a business idea and proposal for him. I am from so and so"* Everyone is looking for an idea because it is idea that sells not really a product. You know why?, it is because a product or service is a by-product of an idea.

V. Do the Discussion as a freelance, or idea base, work force, or the plan you have.

2. Call up anyone you know that can help you with a job opening

Say something like; *I just came out of (school, job, training, etc). I have a plan of starting up (so and so business within six months or so) but I believe I will need some job to gather finances, release some of my potentials and build my vision"*

Do not know why the person you spoke will take you serious and give a quick recommendation whether he knows you are not? It is because you have a vision or plan. He or she now believes you are not the redundant type of person.

No one is looking for someone who cannot perform out stand out. Your propositions as above can give the person the idea of what you are looking for and probably the best.

5. Interview Wisdom

I like to relate what Dr. Mike Murdock shared with us on his visit to Abuja, Nigeria. This may be the opportunity presented because of the above practical section you took. He said; tell your interview or listener this:

"If you give me 4 minutes of this interview, I am satisfied and then offer this four points" I just made it five (5).

1. *I am agreeable and can work with any boss in any department;*
2. *I am corrective because I believe success happens at the speed of correction;*
3. *I take instruction once;*
4. *I complete every task I start;"*
5. *I don't complain but I asked questions a lot. (I added this point)*

With the above tips handled down to people over the internet, Dr. Mike said people called him from all over the world to tell him how successful they have used this wisdom points to find job including those who said initially they were not able to find a job on the surface of the earth.

I communicated these instructions to my beautiful younger sister and she took it gladly. As at the time I wrote this she was working with a financial institution. During that communication, she asked me one salient question: "what if I stop following or doing as I have said or that I could not meet up anymore". Then I simply told her that "it means you have lost that job, you are no longer interested, so get your things and come home". We laughed at that but it was the correct thing and the best way to go about it.

6. Leave Fear alone

Leave fear alone and he will leave you alone. Fear is in-actions and actions with a thought-hold of rejection or failure. But you need to kill it by understanding how and why you don't have to fear? The question 'What will happen if' always call in. Now, knowing how packaged; creative, informed, useful and superior you are, there is nothing like rejection and failure. DON'T EVER BE AFRAID OF BEING TURNED DOWN. The thought and fear of being turned down is the best trick that has killed and held billions of people down. Please don't be among. You know why? If anyone turns you down even annoyingly, it means that person doesn't value good in his life; career or business. Therefore, he doesn't need special creative human beings like you and that is not the kind of people you will wish to work with. Get out quickly...they don't deserve you. You are too important for such place and person or groups. I gave an example, how as a business gentleman, a graduate of B.sc Economics and with my very responsible self and character, I went to a construction site to find something and how to do business with them, but they turned me down. I turned myself up and left quietly even without a feeling of anger or offense because what I know and believe; I know they are not qualified to have me.

What did you hear?

....

....

....

....

....

....

....

....

....

....

....

....

Series Four: How to Start a Media Organization with less than $55

You can start an all encompassing media organization with a computer, or blackberry/Android phone connected to the internet with less than $55 from anywhere. You will be surprised at your profit, strength, idea and discovery. This can work anywhere across the globe. The $55 mentioned here is not to be paid to me or anybody but just a resource you need for some logistics and operations. This technique is actually almost free and powerful and you may not even expend the entire $55 budget before you start making some more cash. What I want to show you is what I discovered after more than 5 years of using the internet.

A media organization is involved in advertisement, research, news, publishing, in print, radio, TV, the internet and the word of mouth. I bare record that how I am able to reach you with this piece I am sharing with you now is all about media. Media is the structure of the Universe and the structure of the media now, is all about the internet.

INTERNET! INTERNET!! INTERNET!!!

I may not want to start bordering you with all the statistics about the exponential growth in internet usage across the globe including in your own country, but the fact is; it is real, massive and accessible. You may have heard but yet to experience the profit. Now I want to teach you a unique way to make you profitable with it. Here you may not need any internet payment system to start with or border people to pay money to your bank account and all of those procedures. I am talking about receiving cash at hand and by hand that can be sooner or later transferred to your bank.

The internet is the bomb to start with. Nobody has a monopoly of what goes on the internet. Everybody is creating one idea or the other that is moving them or their businesses forward and leveraging on the power of the internet to communicate, sell, and deliver effectively and affordably. This type of media business you are about to start is inexpensive but highly creative and can be privately or publicly operated. The internet is expanding by day and thousands of people are coming online daily in one form or the other across the world.

The Idea: Share People, Businesses, Events, Ideas, Products and Services on the Internet.

What you are about to learn works for and can be used for individuals, businesses, corporations and private or public organizations for your profitably. There is no limit to how far you can go. You are only trying to **HELP** them build a positive image, personally, news-wise, product and service wise uniquely on the internet and make them global and sellable.

Media-ship means supplying information from one source to another. Now you don't need to generate any information but help people share their own information exclusively on the internet and may be later offline as well. This could be personal or public events like weddings, launching, induction, etc. Just anything that is sharable about a business or person or organization.

Your Selling Point

You are solving a ***problem*** by ***helping to advertise and build their business and endeavours in a global form***. That is: bridging the communication and advertisement process. They are not helping you but you are helping them create new customer base, link them online for a small negligible amount that other advertisement company would call thousand of figure for them. You are helping because you know how it works and how they can benefit from this. The point is that you are going to go round and meet people especially in their business locations to add them and build for them marketing articles for them, their products or services.

Practical Steps

Step one: Design a plan for a Media Organization or Business by doing one or two of the followings:

    a. Don't start thinking of registering any business name or something. But if you have one, it is ok. And if you are buoyant enough, go ahead. Else, later you may register your business with your proceeds.

b. Create a blog or Website for it. A blog is free, but a website will cost you. If you already have a website, very fine but I will prefer you start with a blog now. Reason is that, it easy to operate, and free to operate. All you need is an internet connection. Use BlogSpot (www.blogspot.com) if you have an internet connection you can see my own here; www.abuja-real-estate.blogspot.com

If you need extra coaching on this, you have to read my *How to create a blog Guide.* Creating and managing a blog is very simple.

Let us say I name by blog; Danik Media. I can say the blog name is www.danikmedia.blogspot.com or just any simple but short name.

If you have created your blog then you are ready to start. Just keep posting the articles daily or as frequent as possible.

c. If you have an ID card or a complementary card, it would be very perfect because it shows some level of seriousness in you for a magnet. It can cost you some few bucks to make from any computer printers.

d. Make a form and print it to describe or collect the information of the person, business or organization you will contact containing; Name, Address, phone contacts, Website, products and services, Events, Other capabilities/Info etc.

Step two: Step out

a. Put on your dancing shoes because the drum is already on. Go out and meet a target; person, business or organization that you wish to publish in their offices, workshops, farms, stands, stores/shops etc. I told you anything (information) goes or works here. It can be someone who has written a book. It can be your work place or club or groups.

b. **GO TO THEIR LOCATIONS**: Meet them at their various locations; speak to them about what you came for: *to collect their information; products, services etc and publish them on your website or blog.* If need be tell them how the internet can help them to advertise themselves and products. And you are offering them a unique opportunity through your media.

Tell them how import this can be for them or their lives, business, products, project or enterprise and that you believed if need be someone will contact them through your media for a better business. Tell them, even if they already have a website, you will drive more traffic to you website through your website or blog site.

c. **ASK QUESTIONS:** You can ask question to help you review a project, profile, event, etc. This can make your review or research news worthy.

d. **TAKE PICTURES**: You can take pictures as deemed fit or permitted with your phone, camera or Ipad. Be smart; do not waste so much time.

e. **UPLOAD THERE:** If you can upload the information there with your IPad, computer/phone or internet connection; go ahead. This will be nice and practical but they can fill the form while you do that later on. Hand them your card. Collect your money and leave. You are pay them more visits.

Step Three: Pricing

a. Tell them you will collect only a certain amount $5-$10 in cash to do this. Don't charge much but use your business acumen to discern how much can be release without much struggle or bargain. You can have a fixed price for particular types of business. You may differentiate price according to business or organization or logistic involved if you have to travel; that is if that kind of deal comes in for you.

b. **Money Back Guaranteed: (optional)**

You may offer something like 'if no one contacts them within one month, they can ask for a refund and you would gladly make a refund.

How easy and free is this. What have you spent? Was it up to $55, and How much did you make? I will love to hear from you on how successful and useful you have been.

Step Four: Use a Group or Partnership (very much optional)

What if you sell this idea to someone else or a group and you run partnership. Hum.... you can cover a lot on grounds or range of business. You can even call this www.YOURTOWNbusinessguide.blogspot.com,or www.YOURNAME.blogspot.com

Etc.

Key: Any functional business works here in this regard and is fit to go online. This is the deal, go ahead. You may even run into a multimillion projects or contract; you are free. Even a beggar can sign up with you if he needs both local and international attentions. Dose this sounds funny?

The internet is the largest market in the world. Not any market in Dubai, London, Hong Kong, Shangai, Lagos, Abuja New York and it is increasing by the day. Apply your own creativity here and stand out; make more cash.

Series Five: Six (6) ways to identify and solve problems as a consultant in any field

A consultant is an expert, specialist, professional, authority, adviser, mentor or counselor in any chosen field or knowledge. It can be an area of your profession, occupation or business. The idea is to impact ideas, creativity, and knowledge for success. For example, in business, they are specialists in small, medium or large enterprise, information marketing, public relations, finance etc. A specialist consultant in agriculture could be offer niche or concentration in yam farming only, animal; cattle or fish farming, or general agricultural support services etc. The idea of consultation is to create, determine and enforce best practices for success.

It may surprise you to know that what really qualify a person or firm to be a consultant is not the certificate but knowledge, success, discovery, experience and training he has and how to use it to the fullness of profit. For instance, you can become a successful consultant by teaching people to avoid the ways that you have not succeeded to concentrate or use where you have succeeded so that they too can be successful.

Build a Solution Mindedness for Profit

We have established that a **problem** is a **seed** for **money** or a **reward**. A problem is a *difficulty, crises, trouble, predicament etc.* A Seed is the *beginning,* or *starting point.* Money is a change in income or a reward for a difference in someone or something. Therefore I can say that a *problem is beginning of being rewarded with money or a substance of value.* Did you remember what we said about being creative in our thinking and actions? Let me give us a reminder of the P.I.S.M formula.

This can be applied to solving problems and challenges. We said your potentials depend greatly on the information you have and how to use it effectively for profit. The information you have can be tailored or determined by the problem you are seeking to or can solve. The problem you can solve (solution you have) determines how payable or rewarded you can be. There is no one on the earth who does not have potential and who cannot have or develop some potential.

Remember **P=I=S=M**

Where **P**=potentials, **I**=Information, **S** = (solutions to problems) and **M**=Money.

Don't ever forget **P.I.S.M** to summarize the fact that a problem is a seed for money or reward. The problem you can identify and/or solve represents the potentials you have. The good thing is that most at times you need to identify the challenge and offer your help-that's another side of creativity. Move towards the problem or someone that has the problem.

Channels of Consultancy and Solution Mindedness/Idea Generation

You can access your consultancy techniques on one or all of the following areas by answering the questions listed below. I want you to use these questions to develop or identify your potentials. You may not limit your mental analysis to the questions that are listed here alone, but it will definitely draw out what you know or can do. We will

discuss 1-6 here and 7-8 later.

1. Where you have NOT succeeded
2. Where you have succeeded
3. Where you have trained or worked or working right now
4. What have you discovered
5. What is not right around you? What is the solution? What can I do or start?
6. Where do you want to succeed next?
7. What your passion
8. What annoys you

1. **Where you have NOT succeeded:** what is your area of challenged right now or before now? How did you get out of it? The area of your challenge is your area of your advantage once you get out. Your area of challenge could be unique to you and benefit to others facing the same or may face it later. What are the ways you tried and failed? Don't allow others to pass through same if you have overcome it. Help them to solve it and so you will be rewarded and solve your own current or next challenges. Do not be ashamed of you non-success areas, it can bring you

success now. Have you seen mind and eye catching titles like these ones below and how did you feel?

(1) 6 Ways I tried but could not find a Job; One best way revealed

(2) How I could not find a wife or husband for 9 years: don't try it.

(3) Why the coup did not succeed in 1959. Don't Try it

(4) 5 things not to do while contesting an Election in Nigeria, America, Australian or South Africa, China and Monrovia if you don't want to fail.

(5) Why you should not to invest in Nigeria oil sector in the year 2015

(6) Why I failed to win Election 3 times in a row; don't make these mistakes.

2. **Where you have succeeded-** sample guide

1. How I won the heart of my stubborn wife; Real Techniques
2. How I left drug, smoke and alcohol in one day.
3. How I got healed of some terminal diseases- a guide
4. How you can mange two wives when the mistake is made and you cannot run away in Africa.

3.   **Where you have trained or worked or working right now:** Wherever you have trained or worked

can be of advantage to other people. They are secrets you may know or experiences you may have that others can pay you for in order to succeed. Whether you have left were you worked or trained or you are still there, you can seize the opportunity.

If you were or are a barber, you be able to answer questions like: 'how to run a successful Barbers' Shop'. If you are into comic relief and masters of ceremony you should be able answer questions like 'how to become a successful Comedian and Public Relations Professional'. Now if you want run such, you can get up and compile some information about it.

4. **What you have discovered**: Discovery is just about being creative to answer questions like what seems new now that needs to be known or what was, and what is likely to be. Discovery is not really about inventing a new thing which has not been

seen or known before now; it can be just about finding a new use to a thing or how to do things differently or unconventionally for speed and success. It is all about adding value to another thing. What is right but can be done creatively to maintained or increase success? Consider the following:-

1. How I found out 95% of people in New York live a fake life.
2. How to identify homosexuals and lesbians by Sight
3. How to come out clean from Homosexuality in 10 days
4. How to be a footballer and succeed in Business in other sectors
5. How to be a musician and business man with a Difference
6. What I discovered in the Life of 90% Musicians that kills: Avoid it
7. How to be an artist without living a fake life or borrowed life
8. Everybody in your community deserve an award- Know how to find them out and reward their difference.
9. Learn how to successfully own an Award winning Award Giving Organization in your Community, Business/Career Sector or State.

5. **What is not right? What is the solution? What can I do?**
Write down at least 3 every month existing problems far or around you that you are passionate about to solve. Write down in you special note book and review this every month.

6. **Where do you want to succeed next?** This section can answer questions of goals and vision and desires etc. What more impact level are you looking at, etc

Assignment:

- Copy this question and make a form with it
- Make 3-5 lines under each
- See if you can answer one or two personally or as a firm. Take 30mins-1hr or day to do this. Skip and answer randomly, you can go off and on...it is ok.
- Keep it, you will know how to use this form to draw out some potentials and information around you and also leverage on it for others businesses.

How to Provide Solutions and Measure your reward

Look for a Reward: Don't fight a battle without a reward. Every challenge is a battle and if solved should bring a reward. Bad times bring good people together because they think alike. An inevitable or unavoidable change is a time to think wide with a focus or vision to succeed.

Your passion: Your Passion can determine where to and what to find solution for. Also, the prevailing situation of your family, firm, community or area or nation can be useful as a breaking point. The difference between you and the rest of the people is that while they are busy talking about the problem, but you are busy asking God for a solution by insight or research or question and answer series like the ones above.

Offer a mind blowing Result or plan: if you are in a 'job needed economy', you can make a unique proposition first to yourself maybe in writing but only for your constant consumption and keep in view, plan or consideration. For example, *'I can make 1 million People employed in one month, 3 months or 6 months or 1 year in my Community, country or the world'.* What you have you is to apply your consciousness and creativity with a constant on the solution and not the problem. Sooner or later; you will find out how or see an opportunity to plan and put your plan to action.

Measuring or Determine a Reward of a Problem.

1. Already Made Reward

I hope you have seen where there is a price tag on a particular person or information if supplied? That is called *already made reward*. Work on this type of problem or related ones, because the reward is clear. Get to the source and ask relevant questions and seek for a time frame to respond, and then work on it more. Be specific in your time so if you can get the solution you can move on to another or to keep the sources in expectation to hear from you.   A consultant can be called to teach and mentor anywhere and paid; you need to position yourself.

2. Measuring your reward by Relationship:

Your reward might first be connection to important personality or organization you can have partnership or have contact with to support your vision or plan. Your reward may not be cash in this moment but can be translated into other opportunities for cash.

3. Fixing you own Reward

The simple fact here is, you can ask for a specific reward as needed or desired for a problem you can solve especially if it is open or if given the opportunity. Competition; music show, pageantry etc don't give quick reward like identifying solution to problems or finding out the problem where and when it is yet to be known and fixing your reward. For example, the prevailing situation and the importance or solution proposition of your book plus prevailing market situation can allow you determine how much you want for it.

Positing as a consultant

1. Build yourself in a particular expertise and be ready to teach or direct.
2. Deliberate search of information and solutions: try to apply yourself to solutions
3. Offer yourself as a Consultant in what you know.
4. Offer help even if free at the beginning or some points
5. Seek to help other succeed

Can you remember something that crossed your mind while you read?

Table Talk: How to Decide & Deploy Creativity in Life, Business and Career.
OKETA, Daniel

....

....

....

....

....

....

Series Six: How to run the Best Award Giving Organization without Cash

There is no one on the surface of the earth who does not like to be recognized in one way or the other for their effective innovativeness, creativity, zeal and effort to better their organization, environment or nation. You can do or offer this recognition perfectly, professionally and build a reward system as a means of awarding excellence publicly or privately.

This is not surprising because all the TV stations in your country for instance can win the TV Station of the Year in the same year but awarded by different organization for different reasons or results. This may be a high example but it works for both lower and higher cadre of businesses, individuals and organizations.

Creative Application Techniques

Now did you remember that form you made and answered some questions from the channels of consultancy and solution mindedness/idea generation? It can be used to start an Award Organization or leverage on your Media business we dealt with earlier. Can you see how connected things can be? Does this sound innovative? Yes it does and I will show you how it can work. You will look over those question and some others you may add and see how effective it can draw other to their achievement and successes for your perfect assessment.

It is better to actually recognize someone or group that successful in an area or business or some sectors genuinely, to pay your respect and earn your own respect also by awarding them. If this is done, substantial reward or beneficial influential relationship is imminent for your efforts. The first attentiveness is to be very watchful with high integrity on your path and others to create value in recognition/award process or determining who to be honoured. You will soon discover some innovative ways to launch out from here. Individuals, Groups, Organizations, and Cooperate bodies can be rewarded or recognized with an award.

One of the creativity here is to build a community, sectorial, people oriented and social support system in general or a particular area. It is going to be simply A SUPPORT SYSTEM, to encourage, build others and reward/recognize efficiency, productivity, consistence and or creativity.

You will need to make your award very much valued, priced or important by obeying the following principles. You may need to work with like minds (one or two persons) in this project. It is important.

Creative Principles for Recognizing Others with Awards

I will list Six (6) main principles of appreciating others in a formal way.

1. **Integrity**: anyone whose integrity is questioning must not receive your award. Make it clear that if someone is selected for your award or even awarded, such award can be withdrawn or such person dis-selected if found wanting by law or become a public disgrace. Write this on your ward guidelines and selection letter. It can be a person or group or association. And you will need to write them and collect your plaque or plate back if that

become necessary or applicable. This will help build consciousness and genuineness of your recognition/award

2. **Target:** The target of the kinds of people for your organizational award is important. Target follows integrity closely. We are talking about channeling of award. You need to target business and social leaders' with visible impacts, creativity, responsiveness more than political or religious leaders and those with educational for their certificates. People make award and give to politicians because they believe they can receive large money from them. I bet you, that is mediocrity, weakness not excellence. Target those who are doing positively as well as trying hard to come up or build positive image in business. You need to encourage them; that's the key. Avoid politicians; they may receive your award and talk-it-away behind you and without respect.

3. **Payment/Fee:** Award are not to be paid for but can be supported in cash or kind by the recipient, groups, organization or individuals. Should someone ask if he/she can pay for it? The answer is *"NO, but your support in cash or kind is very important and desired"*. Never mention a particular amount but you can mention other needs ONLY if on request by awardees.

4. **An Honour:** An award is not by coercion. It is an honour; every honour is either received or rejected. If someone is not interested, fine. Get away from him/her or such organization. Either they don't trust themselves or you. Whichever way there is not trust. They may be interested later.

5. **Competiveness:** Have a List of possible recipients for one award and debate about them. Award should have a list of those competing persons or organization for the same award. Any attempt to just cut awards in different titles for different people must be resisted. An award is not final,

such that if your make your award periodical, there will always be room for others who make improvement to come in. Everyone cannot be reward in a day or year. Sometimes a recipient may ask you how they were selected. Competiveness will become one of your greatest bargaining powers to earn trust.

6. **Periodical:** make your ward periodical and public. Why? It will give others room to aspire and come in later. That someone rejected an award a previous year does not mean he/she cannot be nominated or reconsidered again.

Action Steps

Step 1: Set up a survey with the form you created from our last section. Offer it to individuals or firms on target or just randomly to answer. Tell them it is a research of your company or self-help research as the case maybe. Use what is available.

Encourage and appeal to them to fill it. Tell them it can help them know their achievements or success and ensure focus. You need to move ahead of conventional or traditional ways. None of the questions should be mandatory except names and contact information. This form has the capacity of providing others or responders with a unique way of assessing their lives and even judging themselves. See sample firm below:

....................Your Name of Business Name....................
....

Business and Career Advancement and Impact Research Form

Name...............................Tel/Mobile...............................
Address...
Business or Org Name..
Position...
Website...................................Email.............................

Please Answer As appropriate
1. Where you have NOT succeeded

....
....
....
....
....
....

2. Where you have succeeded

....
....
....
....
....
....

3. Where you have trained or worked or working right now

....
....
....
....
....
....

4. What have you discovered

....
....
....
....
....
....

5. What is not right? What is the solution? What can I do?

....
....
....
....
....
....

6. Where do you want to succeed next?

....
....
....
....
....
....

Thank you for your time and Resources. We will get back to you if need be. *For Partnership, Support and/or Enquiry: Please Call...contact 0980900....*

This form can be used for your Award Reward and you may not even put it forth directly. Now those who will welcome you and definitely take some time, no matter how long to answer this questionnaire are resourceful persons and can be relied on for partnership, Award, and other recognitions like a chance or opportunity to speak at an events or seminars to show case themselves, businesses and worth of experience.

This form may not be more than 2 pages.

Step 2

Evaluate the report and this can determine who should be rewarded with award recognition. This can happen in months so you need to start on time. Write and inform them of their selection and set a date for the presentation. You can get as many as have passed this assessment test you can and conduct the award ceremony at the same date in a public located. Use every media support you can get to inform people on what is happening.

Don't be afraid; it is another way to help yourself and others to succeed; spiritually, emotionally, mentally and otherwise.

Is there any you want to remember or add?

....

....

....

....

....

Series Seven: How to make over 100% in Currency Trading: Not Forex

One of the great businesses is currency trading; but you need to understand how the currency market works to put yourself in an advantage position wherever you may be around the world. Currency trading is generally called Forex and Stock Exchange which can be done on the International online platform or on the platform of any Stock Exchange House. The word Forex is a short combination of 'Foreign Exchange'. This is often complex or just dominated by a group of people who most refuse to show other people the understanding of how things work. My idea is to take you way from this conventional way into a simple but dynamic business procedure that can guarantee profit. I am a sincere Business Consultant, I don't try to sell to people and say they can invest today and make money in millions the next day. I tell you how exponential incremental fortune can only come after you follow the process. Every process takes time with the needed application of techniques in expectation of success. This process can take few months, keep you in business, provide for your needs and yet capable of expanding you into a fortune one day. You will understand this perfectly as we go on.

This is NOT IPOs

One of the worst means of trading stock is Initial Public Offer (IPO) because most times it takes you years (10,20,30) to realize how useful it may become, or even collect your proceeds which are very small in dividend capable of been neglected. At a time in 2012, it was news that the Unclaimed Dividend in Nigeria ran into billions of Naira. They were debating what to use the money for. I don't know where it is now; maybe you can ask your bank officials if you are in Nigeria. You can also offer a research on your own and how to access its use.

I, my Father and including my mother and many others I know had bought IPOs before now. We hardly understand what is happening to our holdings now. And to be sincere, it is nothing worth writhing home about. In fact my father's IPO which he purchased in 2005 did not have a certificate because it seems he was duped by a relative who worked in that bank at that point; who knew the bank was falling in liquidation yet lured him (my father) into buying. For 9 years, my father chased his money everywhere; he almost broke his leg. That's sounds funny? I bet you it is not. At the time I wrote this, he is yet to get his money even his capital N1,000,000 (one million naira) back, that is about $5,291. This happened in 2005; this money could have yielded much if otherwise invested in direct currency trading or other profitable venture. In 2006, I bought an IPO in two sections worth over N35,000 (thirty Five thousand Naira), but up till now am yet to enjoy any profit and benefit from it. I will not say about my mum; whose holdings in IPO is worth about N100,000. Funny enough she used her salary loan-increase as a Civil Servant- too sad. I believe someone reading this has similar experiences.

You should not fall into this again and that is why I am explaining 'what not to do' and 'what to do' with your money in currency trading for the best profitability. I want to make you a local-foreign bank anywhere or country where you are only if you act as instructed here.

This is Foreign Currency Holdings and Exchange.

Holdings in Foreign Currency

It is far better- 100% to hold your money in foreign currency anywhere in the world. The best two currencies to hold your money is the US dollar and the British Pond. Even if you hate these currencies for any reason best known to you, hold it and trade it for your own good and profit.

This is exactly what the banks do to make fortunes. They trade currency and hold foreign currencies. No professional banker will tell you this, which am revealing to you now. Most of the yet-to-be professional bankers simply don't know. Even if you may have access to them; they may just be functioning as some employees who are just enjoying the comfort of working in the bank and earning their pay every month with some commissions and fringe benefits to keep them and family going averagely to focus on their job with a committed loyalty.

There is nothing wrong with that but it can be better, even if you are one of those reading this if you key into.

The banks keep your own money and their own money in foreign currencies and then sell and resell in both locally and internationally markets. This is how and why everyone; individuals, government, corporation who trade money abroad must pass through the banks. The commercial banks will not sell foreign currency to you at official rate unless you are travelling abroad for very reasonable business- health, school, business deals, tourism etc. You are always forced to go to the local sellers. But now you too have to become that local seller with creativity, because you can be able to have or hold your own money in foreign currency as an individual for profit even right in the bank.

Currency Market: Increase and Decrease

Currency market fluctuates on the increase most times but except in times of depression, and yet there is still room for exception.

Let me explain how you access and calculate your gain from foreign currency exchange or trading locally anywhere. For example, US$1 exchange for N180 as at this report in Jan 2015. Before now, 2 months ago,(the fall of 2014) it was going for N160 per $1 for almost the whole year after it rose for N140 and $150. This was the progression, N140, N150, N160, N180. This is in US dollar ($) against the Nigeria Naira (N). You can use your local currency to do this calculation also as it applies to your own country.

The fact is that it will keep increasing and not decrease, trust me and even if it does you must have made your money and switch to another currency because the fact also remains that there must be always be a leading currency in the world economy if one currency collapsed. Here I am even illustrating the official rate, not selling or buying from the local sellers (Black market); that is the term used in Nigeria. The local markets always sell above the bank or official rate.

Nigeria Naira (N) Vs the US Dollar ($)

Most times it is possible to save your money in your local bank in your local currency for months without using them right? But you can yet covert such money into a foreign currency and still have it in your local bank.

Exercise One

Now assuming you had some foreign currency (US $) which you converted from Naira @ N160 per dollar worth of N100,000 only in Nov 2014. That is about $625 only, i.e 100,000/160. And in 2 days you sell $500 to a ready urgent buyer for N165 per $1(that is N5 increment per $), i.e $500 x N165 = N82,500. You can use this to buy again for N162 per dollar. That means your new dollar holdings will $509 i.e N82,500/N162.

Remember you did not sell all your stock of $625 which you had initially but sold only $500. The balance is $125. Now, your old stock ($125) plus your new stock ($509) = $634 as against $625 which you started with but now worth N101,440 only in 2 days.

The next day or say one week later, someone calls up that he or she needs a $600, (I will show how people can know you sell dollar-don't worry). You sell to that person in the local market as the market price fluctuates to N167 per dollar. Price fluctuations are announced or monitored daily usually on TV, radio and newspapers. Now you sold $600 x N167= N100,200. Remember your remaining $34 is still worth N5,678 (i.e $34 x N167).

Now N100,200 + N5,678 = N105,878. You started with N100,000, less than two weeks you gained over N5,000 and could be more.

Question: if your N100,000 were in your local bank in your local currency for 3 months, will it gain a N5000 interest for you? EXPRESSLY NO.

Clue: Don't allow your money to stay seedless or fallow and useless in any bank. Just follow me up still

Exercise Two

Suppose you had N500,000 and you converted it to US dollar @ N160 in October 2014 as it were that is 500,000/160 =$3125. This becomes your trading stock.

But later in December, less than two months even as it became, a dollar ($1) begins to sell for N180. For example, you may sell only $3,000 based on request. That is N180 x $3,000 = N540,000 plus your balance of $125 xN180 = N22,500

That is balance c/d = N540,000 + N22,500 = N562,500

You have made over N60,000 just for keeping your money in a foreign or hard currency as popularly known or called. This could be within a day with your whole money in foreign currency. Therefore it is better off 100 times over to kept and trade your money in foreign currency. The more money you commit the more profit you make even within few hours; and that is how foreign currency trading works for you.

Remember you can trade any currency in this way; Yen, Pond Sterling etc.

Use the Banks: You local banks are not against you trading your money in foreign currency exchange. You only need find out how to; but they won't teach you. They don't even have that time. As I reviewed this piece after three weeks of first penciling it down, the price of foreign currency exchange rate has increased about 0.9%.

1. Withdraw your money from your local bank and change it to a foreign currency preferably US dollar.

2. Open a domiciliary according (optional). Return the same money back to it. Some banks demand two references of same account holder and a $100 credit balance. You can withdraw this in the same currency you dropped it anytime you want.

3. It is not compulsory, you can go collect you money, exchange to a foreign currency say ($) and keep it in your house. But you know this might be risky though.

4. Tell your banker or bank that you sell US dollar. It is not an illegal business. You don't even need to register a business before you start. Go to your local banks currency exchange desk and tell them you sell dollar should anyone need. Give them your contact and collect theirs. In fact they will ask you immediately how much you have. The market is always there.

5. Watch the news. An exchange rate increase in your favour, buyers request or a personal need can make get your money from wherever you have kept it, and sell definitely at profit at the local market. (They always ready to buy just as you would also). Tell them you are a dealer; you have in stock and can sell to them as well as other customers in need. Exchange contacts.

6. You may not need an office now. There is no need of that for a start; you may or may not latter.

Use the Local Traders: There are local traders in every city; get to know them and inform them that you sell foreign currency. Sometimes they may not have enough but direct other customer to you. In fact most times they collect from each other just to meet demands.

Official Bureau D Change (BDCs)

Although there are official BDCs licensed by the Central Banks of Every Country, it may not hinder your business. It is possible and advisable if you could get licensed and registered supposed you can afford this. In Nigeria the Capital Base for BDCs is N35million only about $200,000. The Central Banks provides guidelines of operation and provides more support advantages for accessing and trading foreign currency.

Don't forget: the worst place to keep your money is in the bank in your local currency. You may need to diversify into foreign currency trading; it doesn't matter where you are- in every country or city, this is the same and works perfectly.

Series Eight: How to Start a Waste Management Business with a Unique Partnership

Waste management is very lucrative and very easy to start. We are going to add some innovativeness and creativity to launch you in few months to any future you desire through waste management.

There is wealth in waste- you must have heard this statement before now. But I like to tell you that WITHOUT WASTE, THERE IS NO WEALTH: WASTE IS WEALTH, RUBBISH IS RICHES, and THERE IS TREASURE IN TRASH ONLY IF YOU ARE CREATIVE to find out and operate it.

Understating and Employing Creativity

If you need result and results quickly, you must go creative about everything. This is why I am hammering on creativity, because it takes a creative mind and eye to see the vision, the future and take the advantage by pulling some action. We have talked much on creativity in this piece and it is a core expect and intent in its production and distribution as well as usage. Let me relate another incidence here about personal effect of creativity even in a problematic situation. Problems bring creative thoughts and actions: for instance, even though I had barbed my hair by myself a few times many years ago out of fun or playfulness; I only remembered I could and still did it because I was not disposed to go to the barbers' shop. There is no ceremony I could not have used that hair cut I gave myself. You think this was creative? Yes, I think so too. I also know so many others can do this to shelve their expenses.

Yes it was. In three ways I will show you how: one, I had saved some money, even time. Secondly, I got what I wanted or needed. Thirdly, I learnt greatly. Four, I am telling or teaching you how things can work or made possible out of nothing or in difficult situations so it can benefit and profit you.

Waste Management is a much untapped sector of the environmental economy that can receive local and international support. There is also a mass recycling techniques going round in the entire world. There is a focus on anything that can be renewed after usage. The world is moving towards recycling things to save and restore the climate; and this can translate to cost reduction and more profit for others. What is needed is the supplying of the recycling materials from wherever they may be.

Channeling your Effort

We are talking about a waste collection centre and how to start and management it for profit. This is not to establish a built-million dollar project for a start, but that can come later, you will see that clearly when the time comes. You are not going to be a beggar or one dirty guy or lady running round the street of your city and you may not need to employ anyone to do or start except you want to. Other people should be able to bring the waste products to you, while you get a few others yourself.

The creativity here will work more with a *partnership* and a *reward system* and you may not need to own anything or cash for a start. This will work everywhere in any country. This will help you create the needed attention for support- very important. There is a financial fortune in waste that arises from support and that can be realized in your life and business. You may want to check some statistics of waste recycling around the world using the internet if you need more encouragement.

How to Start:

1. **Discover More:** Do a research on the importance of community and environmental advantage of waste collection and management. Use the internet. This is because you must be able to stand and defend the importance and need of your project effectively before anyone or prospective partners or investors. How you present the project determines how support it can draws. Find out water recycled products you can sell easily and where to sell them in your country and abroad and contact them. For example; *'we are this and that, we do this and that, if we get you this and that, we you buy from us, at how much and quantity can you buy'?* Just do your survey.

2. **Offer to Help/Support:** Always speak from the 'help' side of your business or project to your people, or environment. Offer more to help your community to manage waste. Everybody should have to help one another to be rewarded.

3. **Determine the Products:** you can start collecting iron and aluminum, soft drink and water cans and household, food and cooking cans. Other things like mobile phone craps can be added. These things are easily sold, recycled or needed elsewhere.

4. **Get a Land Space.** Get an empty land or space to collect your goods. It can be inside your compound. If you can get unused fenced land space, it's ok. The place to keep these things should not be a problem since rain and sun cannot damage them, except for a few. If you wish to, make a write up like this; 'Waste Collection Center'. Security is important but not instant until value is seriously harnessed or immersed.

5. **Offer Reward:** Your reward system for those who deliver waste for or to you can work in an effective partnership. What would you offer as a reward? Things that could appeal to children and basically information unique information products like; books and writing materials, Music and Comic CDs, word of wisdom or Gospel CDs. This can be a viable partnership with your church or mentor, individuals, association, club etc such that you will be permitted to reproduce this items cheaply and at will. Add price tags or value t you reward to convey it cost and importance

6. **Partner Hotel and Others local eateries or bars** Contact Hotels, restaurants and bars to separately keep cans for you and your company. Offer them something in return only if you can; not compulsory.

7. **Get online:** Create a blog that tells much about your business, you and ways of helping your community through waste management. Write

and post valuable post and pictures of all that concern the business at least once every week. Look for buyers; find out who needs your products by engaging in search and make contacts.

8. **Offer Freelance:** Now that you are in the environmental sector, try to offer some strategic township or community clean ups for free and create awareness on effective disposal of waste.

9. **Create a Social group of like minds;** to provide support and let them be adequately reward. You can offer them a share or % of profit to work with you.

10. **Offer Consultation:** Offer consultation in business seminars, schools and colleges on how to educate them on waste management and was of effective waste management.

11. **Offer Specialized Cleaning Services:** You can offer specialized mobile cleaning services to public event

places like stadiums, gardens, etc, large corporations, and also other private event venues.

12. **Command attention:** The biggest advantage is that you are positioning to break even with bigger deals. One good deal can keep you soaring high and big for many years. When some or all of the above are in place, you will begin to gain and command attention for positive impact in your life and community.

No one can afford to overlook you. You will receive the needed support. As we said in the beginning, the world is always looking for someone who can take a bold step that everyone can give way to and render support especially in innovative entrepreneurship. Giving a way to you alone is a support done unconsciously that you must leverage on.

Series Nine: How to start a Profitable Real Estate Business Anywhere without Cash

The only thing of the universe in every city in every nation that is capable of appreciating continuously per minutes apart from a Human Being is land otherwise called property. Also, one of the businesses that can change and produce profit over night is real estate. And again, the only thing that transfers 100% ownership of the content and the container is land.

As a real estate trader or dealer, it is not how much you keep a land or house that really matters but how much profit can be made from it per time or transaction. You will need to bring your dynamism into real estate business by being very attentive and passionate about the sector. Let everyone that cares to know get to know that you are into Real Estate. Get perfect knowledge and information about what people may need. The secret of real Estate is LOCATION, LOCATION, LOCATION. Mastering a location is the first thing that matters in the effectiveness and business profitability of any real estate.

Launch Plan

1. **Choose an Area in a City or if possibly an entire City:** Where you want to focus your real estate deals or to begin with? In case you are in a very large city, you can select a particular area because of proximity and accessibility to cut cost to start you business by knowing every little details and available deals. As a real Estate dealer you must be aware of houses and land for sale, including rent variations in your city. Engage purposeful search of your target area of available option from time to time.

a. **Start with Self as a Real Estate Agent:** Begin your real estate business as an individual. I will always emphasis this because a person is a legal entity which can sue and be sued, vote and be voted for. Most business people think they must register a business name before they begin. The creative way is to start with yourself and gets registered later. You need to spend the little you have on the core and how it can multiply rather than otherwise. Get a business card, very simple but beautiful to enforce your credibility and use your house as your business address or collaborate with someone who already has an office for correspondence. Even 10 businesses can be in one location or office; it is all about efficiency in service and being found and located. Call prospective sellers and tell them you are in business as a dealer; buyer and vendor or agent.

b. **How to Get Real Estate Information:** Apart from physical survey. Look in real estate newsletters in your city or selected location. If there is none, start one and others will pay you to get listed. Get listed in local newspapers or church weekly bulletins. This can be used to get potential buyers or sellers.

Get more professional buy searching out yearly government budget of your town or city to know where roads and other infrastructure will be in place so you can advise investors on best options.

c.   **Be Dynamic and Go online**. Create a blog site for your business. Post available properties, and provide other relevant information weekly. Having an online presence is not a joke; it is the real big deal. I need not overemphasize this anymore. Sometime ago, an estate development company got us involved on how to get a mass housing land in another city. That kind of contact can come to you through your blog site or website. I always say start with a blog site, not only because it can be effective but because it comes with no cost apart from your internet access and know-how and it is very simple create and manage. Without an online presence, you are on your own really.

See my real estate blog @ www.abuja-real-estate.blogspot.com

The kind of professional information you can gather and write about will determine how those who come across your blog will contact you. Engage in all advertising techniques that you can figure out; tell your bank, family, friends, colleagues etc.

This can as well be a part time business even though you still have or keep your pay job until you are able to break into a huge deal or stay on your own. Nothing is wrong to combining the two if time permits you.

d.   **Be full of integrity:** Don't try to add-up prices without the knowledge and permission or more so except the request of a seller. Try to avoid all of that unless it is strongly desired by the seller in your reward format or agreement. Communicate your fee clearly which is 5-10% of selling price. Most times buyers and seller pay up 5% each to their agents separately. But most in agents deals in rent/let/lease business, the the renter, tenant bears the total 10% to his agents. In most cases, it depends greatly on the agreement reached before or in the course of the deal.

Developing as a Real Estate Buyer

You are to become a buyer of a real estate (land or house) not actually because you want to live in it but because you want to buy and possibly resell in the next possible hour, day, or month and make profit. This should be your first intention; to make profit. That is why it does not matter how much a property stays with you but the profit you can make from it in the next possible time and move on. You may not need to have any money or all the money. You will need to leverage on prevailing situations, location and price. If you are also involve in one of two of the launch plan described above; it will give you more advantages.

a. **Prevailing Situation**: There are people selling properties everyday for one distress reason or the other. These are the reasons you can leverage on; bankruptcy, someone in quick need of money for another business, divorce or death and family dispute, government auction etc. You did not cause their problems; you only want to help them solve their own problem by buying from them. Look for those who put a post FOR SALE. You need to ask them all the questions necessary; why they are selling. This will help you in pricing well. If it is not a desperate situation, you can slow down because the price might not be right.

b. **Location:** Remember, Location matters first. Your intended deal property must be in a place where you can easily find another buyer. You should know this by how well you understand the economy of your city or development trend and policy.

c. **Pricing:** The price of any property you intend to buy must be 10%-15% below market price. This is to allow you make profit when you put your property in the market the next day.

d. **Target:** Except a buyer approaches you personally and in great need of money, don't look for a choice mighty properties to consider. Search for commercial, rentage properties that may need some renovation or touch to buy for less and can sell for more. The market evaluation should give you this formula. The state of renovation need can determine the price to a favourable position or water the price down to your advantage.

e. **Get your bank Involved:** If you have selected a choice location and got the right pricing below market price, which can be resold easily for profit, then you can write your seller an offer and agree on the price. Also make sure to receive well written reply in agreement of terms. Write your bank or financial officer a request for partnership to purchase such property and share the profit. Attach the offer letter and the reply as well. If it is your sole package without partnership with the bank; tell them to make the purchase on your behalf and keep the papers and your intention of reselling to the next possible buyer. You may need to agree with them to convert the property if you can pay up the loan to a certain time. Remember you have not spent anything yet

Once the purchase is made, and papers transferred to you bank. Put the property back for sale at a slightly higher price. Renovate if possible. It can work better if you into profitable partnership with the bank. Every one like business that could profit them also Resell; make your profit and payback the loan or share profit as agreed. This can work for any viable business land. All you need is to find out if they are in NEED of selling, get the right pricing and location.

Series Ten: How to Get and Sell Information

I believe you have heard that information is the currency of the world. Information sells faster than gold because it is information that sells gold. This means that information is a currency of its own. You know what this means; selling the right information is the best business in the world. In Information and Communication Technology (ICT) terms, those who trade information are called infoprenuers or information brokers.

In as much as freedom of information laws in various countries of the world is key to promotion of democratic participation and good governance through accountability and independent media, it is a major element in private business information distribution and trading but not on the ground of piracy and intellectual property crimes.

KEYS:

1. Get the info First and Offer it; then stand and watch the money come in.

2. There are no overheads and less recurrent expense in trading of information packages. A onetime effort can guarantee life time success.

3. Everyone that needs to succeed needs to know what the biggest successful people know, or has not known.

Sources of Information

You can sell your own information like this book you are reading or other people's information as well. This could be government information on job, business, and health; every sector information that could benefit others in business, decisions or life can be obtained, packaged and sold. I just listed three sources of information.

1. Your Own Information
2. Government Information
3. Other people's information

Your Own Information

Answers to questions like we treated in the section on how to develop your potentials, find solutions to problems and be a consultant in any field can be used to generate your own unique information in many ways. This can be packaged into a sellable material can be packaged and sold successfully. This was how this book was generated and constructed. I will like you to go back and study once more the analysis we used. Let have a revisit on these questions here again with an analysis only on nos 7-9

1. Where you have NOT succeeded
2. Where you have succeeded
3. Where you have trained or worked or working right now
4. What have you discovered
5. What is not right? What is the solution? What can I do?
6. Where do you want to succeed next?
7. Passion
8. Annoyance
9. Creating Right of Ownership.

Passion: you can use your most area of interest, zeal, or excitement. Provide viable ways of getting better and succeeding thereon in order to create the future you desire by teaching or educating others also. Passion can keep you going even if the profit is yet to come or far away but eventually it certainly pays off.

Annoyance: whatever irritates you, you can find solution to or solve. It could be a challenge for you and/or others. That it annoys you also means it does same to some others but they may not have a solution to it or have the time to find out. Information can be build around such areas for profitability.

Creating Right of Ownership; For example pictures: There is nothing that cannot be converted into unique information and sold for profit including pictures. For example, some people have snapped unique, beautiful, educative, inspirational pictures of happenings, animals, environment as such as they are the sole or original owners that could be turned into a fortune. Some of this people ignorantly turn it to social media and loose the intellectual property right. I tell you that such unique pictures can be framed and millions of copies sold with full intellectual property right. News companies and many others media organization buy pictures and pay for right of use picture for news and publications. You mobile phones or cameras can turn you into the next millionaire through picture creativity.

Clue: Never dwell on negative things but those that can inspire people to greatness. If it inspires you, it can inspire another.

Government Sources

Now your discovery can be from government information that could help a particular group of people. Sometimes these could be legislation of rights and privileges, access to community or social funds; loan, grants, business, education, scholarships openings etc year in year out. They are all free to access and republish without any legal implication of intellectual property right. If you don't know; today you have known. I heard from someone that the largest source of information is the world is the US government. That could be very true and can be tapped through the internet. The government of a particular country could possess information also that can be specific to various regions or areas of national development, business and personal growth.

Other People's Information

Taking advantage of other peoples information is far from copyright and or piracy; it is a way of acknowledge people world for the benefit of spreading their successful impact and making others more successful.

For instance, people have packaged others best quotes in frames and into books etc and have made fortune out of thin air. I have read of someone who collected some great quotes over time. He and his wife decided to compile some and send to friends and family as Christmas gift. They met a printer and a price and amount was agreed. But there was a gap in the communications and 1000 copies was made instead of 100. When the bill came also, it was $10,000 dollars instead of $1,000. They ended up selling all the other copies and made tremendous profit over and over again because I believe yearly they would have to come up with different quotes.

Clue: This opportunity still exists today; some quotes can be documented in audio Cds or MP3s and sold or distributed to the right audience.

How to Begin or Build Consciousness as an Infoprenueur

An Infoprenueur is someone who markets special information, reports, researches or secrets. Consider the following ways a means of building a successful career as information broker.

1. **Positioning:** Position yourself as someone who can find out information on anything and work towards it. Be interested quietly in information generation; reading, listening or purposeful research. The tiny sentence of anyone can be worked on and turned into spinning money information. For instance, I made a statement while I was treating the business of currency trading that: I don't know where the Unclaimed Dividend of IPOs in my country is. Someone can pick that up for instance and start a purposeful

research on how individual and firms can reclaim their money which may have been laid unprofitably for more than 10 years.

2. **Offer a Niche.** You can tailor your information to your area of expertise, training or job. There are many things you could know that beginners, newcomers in your industry do not know. They can pay you to obtain it in order to fast tract their entry and make them more successful.

3. **Offer Information that Provide Advantages:** Apart from well tailored requested information and search, offer information around what gives people advantage; for example, that saves or can generate more income. The key is to provide SOLUTION, INSPIRATION AND SUPPORT.

The Five Ring of Riches for All Infopreneuers

Robert G. Allen, Author of the Multiple Streams of Income and Internet Income uses the above to discuss vast opportunities in the information building and market as:

1. Succeeding in your Core Expertise

2. Teaching Others Specific Know-how to Succeed in your core Enterprise

3. General know how (teaching others success keys)

4. Database Marketing to your core list- partners, joint venture etc and

5. Support Services to Infopreneurs.

I would like to throw my personal light on number 5, which is Providing Support Services Infopreneurs to the first four opportunities. What support services mean here is to provide the necessary expertise to those who may have information, make them successful in order to be successful. The following are some of the potential support services listed by Mr. Allen:

1. Printer

2. CopyWriter

3. Audio Producer

4. Editorial Services

5. Mailing-list broker.

6. Graphic artist

7. Ghostwriter

8. Speech coach

9. Literary Agent

10. Venture Capitalist

11. Infomercial producer

12. Informarketing coach

13. Video Reproduction and CD Duplication

14. Advertising Agency

15. Public Relations

16. Book Reviewer

17. Researcher

18. Information broker

19. Computer strategist and

20. Website designer

Now as you read through this list; what did you identify you can do or developed interest in to support other peoples information or further the course of your information provision technique and support the information industry? With any as any more of the above in place, you have a place to share in the information profit growing industry by opening up a partnership with those that have information products.

IN THE INFORMATION INDUSTRY, WE CREATE AND CHANNEL AND PROVIDE SUPPORT

"Nothing Happen by accident in the world of computers, the Net, and customer response. There is always a reason for what happens, happens good or bad, and that reason is you" – Ken Evoy.

Series Eleven: How to Self-Publish Your Book for Profit

1. What you are willing to write down determine how important or valuable it is. That means you can create real and sustainable value from your writing.

2. What you are willing to write down determine how long you want to keep it or remember it. Even songs are written down so they can be sang correctly.

3. What you are willing to write down determine what others will read, if they have to.

4. The future is a product of what is written down.

5. Something you write down determines what you will see, remember and work with or apply by yourself.

6. Something you can write down determines what confidence you have in yourself and on that which you wrote.

7. Your write-up determines your authority and the confidence of others in you.

By yourself individually, you can publish books, e-books, music, images etc without strenuous approval approaches or other forms of discouragement from traditional publishers. In the world of publication and media, individual/independent (indie) Publishers or self-publishers means you can eliminate publication hindrances by creating your own content and offering it directly or indirectly for sale both electronically (e-book) and otherwise. The most important aspect which you need to handle here is that you get your content right and well edited even by yourself or with assistance. E-books; electronic versions of your work can be delivered online anytime. You can successfully have both paper back and E-book version running for you.

Where Does Books Come From?

Writing or books spreads through a lot of ways; thoughts, expectation or fiction/imaginary tales, experience, secrets, tips/guides, storey line, adventure etc; i.e. just anything good that can bring more idea, teach or build others, bring them more profit, minimize their cost, achieve more and/or inform or inspire the next person. For instance, a good number of people have put things down for their personal use and help at first but later turned it into a big money making venture. This means that at first, they had themselves in mind and not the public, but they offered it and it become very useful or encouraging for others who willingly paid to have it. If you have a passion for writing; then you must find out how to improve and explore it for a career, profit and business.

Starting as a Writer or Author

Writing can be of great profit if innovatively carried out and marketed. Writing should not be a one-off thing, because numerous ideas and happenings come daily or regularly that needs to be documented and released from one part of the world, society, business, career, and life to another. New and advanced techniques of achieving things are always replaced from time to time which needs to be communicated or transferred. Also, old books need to be improved upon, promoted and new books have to come onboard in as much as you also need to promote yourself and build more success strategies. Writing is so self-motivated and dynamic that fully employed people can succeed part time or full time and still build their vision. For instance, if you are into fiction/creative writing/imaginary tale, you can imagine how you want things to be like or act like in the future and structure it into a book now.

Type of Publishing

1. Conventional or Tradition Publishing
2. Self Publishing
3. Hybrid Publishing

1. Conventional or Tradition Publishing:

Conventional or traditional publishing involves getting to a publishing company directly or through an agent, submit your manuscript which they may reject or accept to publish your work. If they do accept, they make you a deal with some stringent conditions. Some major features of conventional or traditional publishing is that they determine if they will publish for you or get your book in the market; online or offline in bookstores depending on the publisher. They also determine the price of your book. Here the company has both bookstore and digital rights of your content; because most time it means you sold it to them as they often pay you in advance.

2. Self Publishing/Independent Publishing

In Self-Publishing, you are the major determinant whether your work or book is good enough to be published or not, you set the price, the title, design etc; therefore, all successes or mistakes is traced to you. Mostly and significantly all these are done online and delivered electronically in E-book form. You can handle self-publishing from the comfort of your home or office with an internet connection and your electronic book (E-Book) is ready for sale to millions of people around the world. Many channels or companies offering self-publishing services offer print-on-Demand in paperback to the author as well as other customers on request. E-book and self publishing can get you paid daily, monthly or quarterly based on the company involved. Through the power of the internet; self-publishing your work or book or information product is not as difficult as having the right product and knowing how and where to publish it to guarantee profit. This is because the tools are basically simple to use.

Hybrid Publishing Deals

This is somewhat the combination of the conventional and self-publishing rights for a publisher although this is just becoming a reality now; that is, to get your book in electronic format on sale as well as a deal for bookstore availability. This means an independent publisher can be offered a print-only contract-and a significant pay advance by a major publisher while still retaining the right of his e-book version on sale online. This kind of deals mostly comes after the huge success of an E-book sale with great potentials of more sales. It can be such a good deal also for a publishing company because there are serious risk and uncertainties involved in publishing a fresh book and making it available in bookstores; but if they can stumble on a deal to print an already bestseller that is self-published online (E-book), then a lot of risk is eliminated.

The advantages of hybrid is that you (author) can be offered a huge advance by the printing company, and you maintain your self-published right. This means a great royalties from the dual rights of the self-publishing right (E-book) and the print-only deal availability at bookstores and libraries. Also, you may still set the price of your piece so that it is not over priced.

These kinds of deals are rare but they are coming around now as a way to leverage on the transformation of the traditionally publishing media through the internet and with self or independent publishing. If your e-book succeeds so well, you will definitely get an offer of a double deal right. This was the experience of **Hugh Howey** who made over $150,000 monthly (20,000–30,000 copies p/month) from his e-book (Wool) alone. Expert in his Jan 2014 interview with entrepreneur.com titled **"How Hugh Howey Turned His Self-Published Story "Wool" Into a Success"** is out outlined below:

Question: You were having fantastic success through e-book sales alone. Why take Wool to a traditional publisher?"

Reply: *"When I hooked up with Kristin (an agent), we discussed the fact that there was very little chance we would actually sign a deal with a traditional publisher. They would want the digital rights, which was how I was making a living, and they would want to take the [e-book] down. It could take a year before I saw any sort of payment, and I was getting paid monthly [at the time]. So we had these conversations [in order to] get publishers used to [ideas] they were uncomfortable considering, and we figured it would help some author years from now. ...*

Finally, Simon & Schuster came up with a contract that was everything we were looking for. It was a print-only deal, [and there was] nothing to hamstring my self-publishing career. They embraced what I was doing on my own and they just wanted to offer this book to a wider market. ... And it's gotten a lot of attention in the publishing industry. Another author, [Colleen Hoover], has [since] gotten a similar deal, so that's exciting to me".

Staring as Self-Publisher or Independent Publishers

According a US based research in 2014; there are six (6) million self-published books every year. This is even encouraging because it tells you to stand out on your own with your book or ebook. A book is a mark of authority and success in your area of specialty or knowledge and an opportunity to add another stream of income to your life. As a writer if you want to succeed and succeed well, you need to continue and keep going, keep learning and writing; as Frank Lloyd Wright would say:

"I know the price of success: dedication, hard work, and an unrelenting devotion to the things you want to see happen."

For me personally, I have decided to use at least 2 hours every day for my learning vision and to compile my insight as write-ups. It can work for you also if the passion is there or simply make do an opportunity by getting involved with a routine of your duties and desires. I have heard and also believed that: *"routine can take you to any future your desire-* Dr. Mike Murdock.

Find out some few ways to muster courage into self publishing and succeed.

1. **Decide to be a writer and an author:**

   Put your ideas together with a plan to make it into possibly a book; novel or inspiration or something worth reading about. Research has shown that about 81% of those interview believed they have at least one (1) book inside of them. I believe personally that everyone has at least five (5) books inside of them.

2. **Decide to start with self publishing:** Start with self publishing now. Instead of keeping your manuscripts in the drawer, bring it in to self publishing. Bring as many as you can; because in the business and world of writing, we may never find out how important we could be to others unless they get to see or read about what we know or think. Self publishing is costless and you have all the tools to sell your idea once you can get online. This in simple terms is getting your work available for sale online as E-book: With an e-book, there's

no printing, nor over-printing, no need to forecast, no recurrent expenses, no lost sales due to out of stock, no transportation costs, no warehousing costs, and there is no secondary market such that e-books are not resold as used books.

3. **Get your right content and work with it.** Get as much content as possible but get it right and well edited and presented. Most times for some information writers, you can package as many information together of a kind and make it available as one piece. One write-up may not do you much good or make you rich; and you may even need to add and update some for better progresses. Your work must be well edited, such that you don't turn a potential lead generation for great recommendation off. If you can manage it; hire an editor or get help from your network to scrutinize your work. .

4. **Set your price aright:** You will need to set up your price right now to be over priced. In fact it is better to be underpriced with more sales than to be over priced with lover results. Try as much to stay in the range of $10 for an e-book (an industrial advice and campaign anyway). But it still depends how important you think or believe your information is worth. Most self-published books die because they set their book on high price; don't get into this trap.

5. **Go ahead and Market**: Even if your book is best in the universe, marketing is a must if you want to grow, maintain it and realize all the benefits. Engage in many low cost or creative advertisement medium as much as possible. You can hire social media marketers to market your books. You need to work around social media and other online channels to promote your inspiring books or ideas that can help others and their environment. You should also use offline medium. For example, in as

much as you have a presence online on the internet; you are also physically mobile offline.

6. **Launch your book:** Launching does not necessary mean; you must gather people in a particular location. You can create a launch if your book is ready or already published by setting a date to announce to everyone everywhere with short massages or review of your new book. Try to reach at least 100 people and ask for the review or comment on your book as short as possible. Use your network and offer the book as free gifts to them as well.

7. **Get a Review or Constant Review:** Purposely ask for a review from all who have read or bought your books. Review is very important, if your get a good review from a good source or widely accepted author or individual, it well help rank your book high leading to more attention and possible sales.

A good review shows that your book is worth reading or buying.

8. **Join a Team to support one another:** This is very important; support one another. Books can never be the same exactly; thereby a book can exist on its own without negatively influencing the chances of others. You can join the team of content writers, advertisers, entrepreneurs to write together, review together, promote together, share ideas and share profit as well. Once we share more, we spread wide and spend less time for other valuable use. You may never know how important you book or title is until you share it with others especially those with the same passion who know the value of writing or books in general. For instance, individuals may send out title for reviews and get minimal or no reply at all; but a group can escape such hurdle; because everyone is involved.

Getting Involved with Independent Publishing Companies

There are so many self publishing companies and you need to be careful to select that which could offer you a good option and terms for success. I did a search on Google and found about 25 of them but very few appeared creative enough for start-up entrepreneurs and individuals with less cash and to leverage on. I analyzed and checked them up; amongst which I selected *'CreateSpace'*, *'Kobo Writing Life'* and *'IngramSpark'* with little exposition in order to only provide some examples.

1. Working with CreateSpace

I picked CreateSpace (owned by Amazon) as one with a creative approach; it is free to start and finish until your book sells and earns you royalty to share some part with them. Other companies require you to pay for startup and other fees. By Using CreateSpace, if your book doesn't sell, you do not owe anyone, you are dept free and you did not pay to start after all. Therefore, if you need to test your work or creativity online with self or independent publishing without paying, CreateSpace is best for you. Your commitment is largely with your write up, and internet connectivity where you are. You are not forced to submit your manuscript for review; expect you want to pay for editing. You do everything yourself and let you book out online and possibly offline based on Print-on-Deman. CreateSpace also offer Audio book and music self publishing in this same manner.

The following are the summary of what I believe you need creatively that CreateSpace Offers:

1. Create Account (Free)
2. Design and upload book, publish, distribute online (free)
3. Set your price. (CreateSpace campaigns or advices for lower e-book price not more than $10)
4. Your book continues to sell as e-book through Amazon.
5. You can get a Print On Demand (POD) if you need it for any reason. Cost of printing and shipping is accessed form cost of the book not borne by you.
6. You get charged some percentage as processing fee on sale of each book. You can earn up 70% in many categories of sales combined.
7. You own the digital right.

8. International Standard Book Number (ISBN)
9. Expended Distribution through Amazon: online retailers, bookstores, libraries, academic institutions within Unites States only.

2.   **Working with Kobo Writing Life:**

Most of the CreateSpace features apply to Kobo Writing Life.

3.   **Working with IngramSpark,** (operated by Lighting Source). As any example, here, there is set up fee with yearly fees although with many other benefits. The table below shows the set up fee as at **Jan 2015:** accessed through IngramSpark website.

Title Set-Up Fees	U.S	U.K.	AU	EU	CAD
Print & E-Book (set up simultaneously)	$49	£29	$53	€36	$53
Print Only	$49	£29	$53	€36	$53
E-Book Only	$25	£15	$27	€19	$27
Market Access Fee (To Ingram distribution channels)	$12	£7	$13	€9	$13

Also, see IngramSpark's **Global Market Access fee for Book & E-book Distribution.** According to IngramSpark, you can make your titles available for purchase to over 39,000 global retailers and their consumers come with the following global market access fees (Retrieved Jan 2015: IngramSpark website).

1. **Book and E-book Market Access -- $12.00** per title, per year (if submitted at the same time)
2. **Book Market Access -- $12.00** per title, per year
3. **E-book Market Access -- $12.00** per title, per year

Create, Sell and Manage Yourself

You can create, sell and manage your book by yourself as a company or individual publisher. Here you need to obtain your International Standard Book Number (ISBN) by yourself through the local branch your country that is the National ISBN Agency of the International ISBN Agency. You will need the ISBN to be able to market your books locally and internationally. It may cost you some money and how much is usually based on the county involved. You may as well submit your book with other online business firms like Amazon (through the Publisher Section) for more sale and business.

Creating and selling yourself takes some level of knowledge and tools that you can handle by yourself effectively. This means you can sell directly with or without listing elsewhere. And again selling directly may mean you need to use your payment system or integrated on your website, supported by your financial institution or an online payment system to receive your proceeds. You may need to be really established already as a name or brand to make more impact here through this medium.

Series Twelve: Understanding and Accessing the Powers of the World

In 1980, the world population was just above three (3) billion but in 2014, it stood at about 7.6 Billion. That is more than 50% increase in thirty five years: Does this mean that in 2040 it will be over 14 billion people on the earth? Time will tell. Where do you want to be among this number dead or alive?

The challenge many people face is not of location, it is how to profit from their location. Therefore the challenge is not really the occurrence or lack of circumstances; it is the knowledge of how to prosper from the circumstances that is needed. This is why two people can be in the same condition, environment, house, womb or school or city etc and achieve many different results; where some fail woefully or succeed minimally, but others succeed tremendously. Character plus knowledge creates or produces a destination. Welcome to the power of difference, planning, consistence, imagination, system, words and of God. Learn how to use them for your prosperity.

1. The Power of Difference and Time

What is in vogue or trendy may not always be what is right for you personally and otherwise. The world works by difference; differences in circumstances, locations and personalities which must be understood and used for profitability of the soul and body of mankind. This difference rest on creativity and usage; and this is why no two persons have the same finger print around the Universe. For example, if everything is the same, then nothing can work effectively. The system of the world is subject to a pattern of general believe or lifestyle; you will need to live above it in goodness to succeed. Time changes by providing opportunities for all who would take it.   Find out below how the responsibility, knowledge and time powers difference around the world:

a. **Responsibility Powers Difference**: Responsibility means doing things differently, creatively or uniquely to power up success until it becomes a habit visible to the eyes and can be perceived. Responsibility makes us want to succeed against all odds. Until you succeed, no one needs to or will want to hear from you. When you succeed, your result speaks before you arrive and when you arrive, everyone is quite to listen to a voice of a great person. I heard that some university students caught up with their proprietor and asked him what he uses that he achieves more, while them; the students take all sought of things not to sleep in order to read? The man answered and said 'I take responsibilities'. For me I will advice you; take responsibilities and also take all what you need to take in order to remain awake and get your responsibility achieved or done. Start leaving in the realm of 'I finish every task I begin'.

b. **Knowledge powers difference**. Millions of people who have gone ahead of me know things that I need to know to help me run or possibly fly. The operation of knowledge often suspends the economic law of intrinsic value. The law holds that the higher the value of a product, the higher the price. But the price paid to get wisdom and knowledge is drastically lower that the value; difference and reward to be obtained.

c. **Timing your Knowledge or Difference:** I agree that knowledge gives or makes power; but I tell you, the first power you have is time. It is by time that you get knowledge. What are you using your time for? Therefore, *time* equals knowledge and equals *dominion*. Dominion or power is what we know and the time we know it and can use it. Time cannot be separated from dominion because what we know determines how long we can hold one, press on and persist. For example if I know about a gold mine in a large place FIRST (time), I will acquire it before you know later- (time). Time fuels discovery and discovery is a more personal force driving a person into action. If someone is close to you, what you eat cannot enter into his/her belly; therefore most times you need to discover for yourself for recovery. That is why ignorance is the highest form or level of witchcraft or hate a man can silently or unnoticeably inflict on himself. How you manage your time determines what you will know and the difference you can create. Time is best managed with routines, because routine can take you very far into the future.

Secure your Place and take position of your time: The first place to secure in your house is not the sitting room, living room or kitchen; but the study- it can be a table and a chair with a lantern to start with and all other things will follow. Someone screened the following to my hearing and it has never left me *"Life is indeed is short, but the times and seasons that come with life are shorter. What have you down with your time?"* Have you been using your time well? Your time is your greatest opportunity. If you don't take the opportunity of your time now, it can easily be wasted. Today's energy and resources may not be there tomorrow.

d. Learn by Instruction: There are two ways of learning: knowledge by experience and experience by knowledge. Literally the first one means; what you know channels your experience while the second means that you are much more taught after or by experience. The second causes more harm than good. The former is the key or the best; i.e to learn by more and more instructions for better results and successes. In order words, I am saying that instructions should fuel or result in experience first for quick and maximum impact such that the experience becomes channel for creating gain or profit once and many more times. The way of instruction is to avoid calamity. Wisdom or instruction brings wonderful or exponential results, saving time, energy and resources. This is daily and constant; you know why? The knowledge of today can be the mediocre of tomorrow. If everyone knows the same thing you know- It means you can hardly excel or achieve anything more than them. And if that is the case then where and what is the difference in you? Also, if you don't act, you cannot know how differently you can survive or succeed. Many secretes that great people would not or could not share are written down in their books.

2. The Power of Association

The best association or corporation is one most important key to greatness and success in life and business. If you believe what I believe and know what I know, there is nothing we cannot do or nowhere we can't go even together. The less your wrong association, the less your accusation and likewise, the less you talk the less your errors, mistakes, inaccuracies or exposure. I had someone who always wants me to join him in his business plans or ideas. Each time we met, he tells me his ideas and how I need to join him. But the case with him is that he never accepts my own plan or idea as workable. What do you think right now? I think he is trying to use me only to achieve his plans alone. If not so, he would believe me and see how we can partner or combine both of ideas for success. A good partner believes in you and your ideas; and always seeking how to rope it with his or hers.

No one owns a bank; the leading owner may only have the largest share capital. Most banks are successful because they are always in partnership synchronizing their ideas for profit. A corporation, partner or an organized business group will be able to realize its foundation and become very efficient for all those involved to release their potentials and realize their own vision. Anyone willing to toe this line must first understand our fold concept. A fold is something that is over or round about each other; that binds or holds something mutually. It is can be said to be collection of many things of particular kind. It pulls strength, or force, energy, ideas and resources for better and higher achievement or influence.

3. The Power of Commitment and Consistence: the creative Approach

Starting anything is not fun; it is usually rigorous because of the huge result or impact that is expected. But the fact is, there must be a start or a beginning. If you are a committed and consistence person, then you must be creative about your start up in order to maintain force. Being creative here means maximizing everything you have in determination; it starts with time and energy then financial resources.

Commitment means given it all it takes in order to receive all that it carries. Commitment can be in *time*, *energy* and resources. The result of all three level commitments geared in one place or thing can bring substantial result. Commitment is released effectively with an expectation for a higher reward or result.

Commitment is powered by consistency. Consistency is the schedule, plan or routine involved in achieving a thing. For instance, going for lunch break every day between 2pm-3pm is a plan or schedule meant to rejuvenate, resuscitate and strengthen you for higher commitment to your duties. Also, planning, reading and meditating everyday for 2 hrs between 12am-2am for example is a consistency or plan of commitment. Your plan fuels, channels and releases your commitment. Once is never sufficient; that is why persistence or consistency is the cure for all forms of resistance. Plans are to be followed but not rigid; it can change based on assignment, location or circumstance.

4. The Power of Planning or Vision

A vision is not a night dream or a dramatic unconscious experience but a physical visible mental picture that orders thoughts, actions and even night dreams for a goal. A vision is a plan showing that there is desired level of responsibility or concern. Responsibility is the key to solving personal or public problems and obtaining a reward. A vision or plan creates an internal readiness or consciousness from the outside which can become tangible. There are three phases of creative vision exemplified below:

1. **Outside to Inside:** Picture of a car on paper; cost, and where to get it

2. **Inside to Outside:** Character, behavourial pattern based on expectation of 1

3. **Realization:** Car purchased and in use tangibly.

Phase 1: this is where you create a mental picture of your desire and need by planning. This plan is usually written down and/or picture and put in front of the eyes. This is the communicative or conduction law of Vision: A plan or vision is targeted first towards the eye for a transmission to the brain (Central Nervous System) from where signals are sent to all parts of the body for a need. This means that what you see you can take-in or get pregnant with. It is only what you are pregnant with that you can deliver. Therefore as many things as possible in a day, your plans or the future you seek to see must cross your eyes.

Your plans or visions are your request. God brings perfect opportunities once your motive is right. A hope is a plan; those who have hope have plans; written and pictured for action. That is why a hope is not abstract, it must be seen. God's mercy is a function or product of the hope or our expectation in Him

Phase 2: You must succeed first from the inside because a vision brings or creates genetic transformation from the inside to the outside. This is the magnetic attractive or compelling law of vision. This can also be known as the developmental stage to maturity. The constant eye capture, thought focus and review of plan in **phase 1** does the following:

1. Order behaviour or general life style in spoken words, walk, and posture or positing in expectation of the realization of plan.

2. Magnets and identifies opportunities for the realization of plans and vision. The eyes have a magnetic capacity that binds objects to memory for remembrance and appropriate action and strength to the body. This means that what you are committed to is committed to you. What you are aware of is aware of you. What you hates, hates you. What you appreciate comes close to you.

Phase 3: This is the maturity time or realization of plan of vision. It is the delivery point. From this point another cycle has began in the use of your product(s); appreciating and maintaining same to birth another future by relying more on what the process that brings you success.

5. The power of the System of Process

A system is a structured pattern; a process is the steps involved in the System. God works in a process and that is how He has designed the Universe to function. This is why the Universe turns round and round continuously in a circle. A man who wants to flow with the universe and achieve success must understand and follow the process required for what he wants or his vision. Since the world rotates; if not for supernatural influence of God's miracle, once you miss an opportunity in point A, you may have to wait for it the next time the Universe will turn it to you again.

Processes are principles that guarantees reliable, sustainable and definite outcome. For instance, God's promises are sure and very certain or concrete but are programmed. If the process and program is followed carefully, nothing can resist the result. The time and processes involves is our actions in expectation of the promises demonstrated in character; spirit and 'make up' until we possess the outcome. The word 'make up' as used here is how to program or schedule things deliberately to work in our favour.

A system is a principle built on *readiness*; *accuracy*; *usefulness*; and *understanding* of need process or outcome. A system is that principles of order by which confusion is rendered impotent and impossible. What have you mastered or determined to do? Have you structure-rized the time; because Day and night must be structure-rized for efficiency. Have you routine your life and endeavour? A system or structure of any process can be hardly ruined or destroyed but can rather be built upon.

If you are ready, what do you seek to know daily? If you are accurate, what is your scheduled? If you are useful, what solutions do you seek to provide or what do you need? Do you understand the process, do you know that your reward is in the solutions. What do you expect and at what intervals do you expect them? For example, in every successful school or educational system; the system of learning is motorized by a time-table. This is applicable to the school of thought or life; which must be powered with a time-table. Your life's time-table could change very month or quarterly. Don't be rigid with it because assignments change with time. God will not find the solutions to your problems for you. He knows the solution; you can decide to find the solution and He will graciously and mercifully reveal it to you.

6. The Power of Mastering Your Words

We water our picture-vision or plan (plant) by the words we speak. A lot of people think it is only when they keen down or stand-up in prayers that their words become effective. Wrong and negative words have been one of the greatest abusive ways of living in any man's life on planet earth and beyond. That you must speak and speak only right, is not a choice if anything is to go well with you. There is no joke in speech; what you say stands and mean at all times. So many people have killed their visions and plans from manifesting because of their negative words. Your speech is the watering of your plans for actions or opportunities. You level of watering matters how much yield or result you will see. I have heard of someone whose Fever of Unknown Origin has be diagnosed to the negative words she used on herself. Once she stopped, the deadly fever with cure left.

Exercise: fetch water in your palms, put it in your mouth for 2-3 seconds and return it back directly to your palms again. Do this about 3-4 times. What do you notice? The water from your mouth back to your palm becomes hotter than it was. This means fire; therefore you can burn and destroy everything good that in your life, business and carrier by your words. Have you also noticed that the tongue is never burnt but only our mouth tissue does when we eat hot substance? This means that the tongue has the capacity to bless also, cool, calm things down or and speaks life. If your words are not right, your life and endeavours cannot be right.

From this day till death, watch all you say; if it is not given life then it is killing a life of something because there is no middle ground. Monitor your speech as you would stop an oil stain on your white neat shirt. After the day's job, outing or work, sit back and think about all you have said or spoken today. Do this for three days only and master it. Your words shape your world; it doesn't matter where you live. That you watch your word does not make you a saddened, smile less, introvert person, it only means your guide and channel you words very right, to you self, your situation, others and everything around you.

7. The Power of God

The power of God supersedes and overrules all other powers. We need not over emphasized this; because it is through God that all powers can be accessed without errors. Everything that is available to a man is owned by

God; therefore get connected to God in uprightness and

with an action based plan or desire to know and operates

in the fullness of excellence.

Series Thirteen: The Eight (plus One) Pillars of Prosperity

I have come across most of the published meticulous work of James Allen, the acclaimed greatest inspirational writer of the Twentieth Century. In his commendable write-up, The Eight Pillars of Prosperity; he dealt with Energy, Economy, Integrity, System, Sympathy, Sincerity, Impartiality and self-reliance in such order. After reading through a few of this title even though I have previously read his most sellable title: As a Man Thinketh, I went over this time to read about his bibliography. I found out that this is the man has mentored many through his inspiration write-up. According to the Bibliography, his work touched many of the twentieth century's leading writers of motivational thought, including Norman Vincent Peale, Napoleon Hill, Robert Collier and Dale Carnegie.

But I notice one striking feature about James Allen that I was not very comfortable with; first he died at the age of forty seven and was not widely know during his life time. Now, what can kill a man, which wrote a mastery of thinking or thought; was he thinking and ready of dying at forty seven? I believe forty seven is a very early age to die of a man with such an in-depth analysis. As I looked further into James Allen eight pillars of prosperity I discovered one pillar was missing. That is why I re-titled it as The Eight Pillars (plus 1) of Prosperity. The one I added is not the last but now the first as numbered below.

The Eight Pillars (plus 1) of Prosperity

1. **God-Reliance:** (Spiritual Chain of Authority, Partnership, Dependence) Oketa, Daniel
2. **Energy** (promptitude, vigilance, Industry, Earnestness)
3. **Economy** (Moderation, Efficiency, Resourcefulness, Originality)
4. **Integrity** (Honesty, Fearlessness, Purposefulness, Invincibility)
5. **System** (Readiness, Accuracy, Utility, Comprehensiveness)
6. **Sympathy** (Kindness, Generosity, Gentleness and Insight)
7. **Sincerity** (simplicity, Attractiveness, Penetration, Power)
8. **Impartiality** (Justice, Patience Calmness, wisdom)
9. **Self-Reliance:** (Decision, Steadfastness, Dignity, Independence)

The God-Reliance: When you are God reliance, you need to pattern your first prosperity pillar on complete dependence on God through partnership and honouring your spiritual chain of authority. The spiritual chain of Authority includes; honouring God with the tithe, Honouring Parent and family, honouring Spiritual head or mentorship. This forms a perfect form of corporation and synergy that transmits honour. Dependence in the God-reliance pillar also is the continuous desire to know and experience God directly by oneself through the His word. This will form or expose a man's own uniqueness, or class since everyone has a different finger print in the entire universe even with the case of the most identical twins.

The Money-Seed

Every money is a seed and a seed has the right, and capacity to be multiplied over and over again but only if sown. It doesn't really matter how small or big the seed is. These principles are simple and purely God's principles. God is the source and can sustain our investments. I believe the best way God helps a man is to tell or give him instructions on what to do, how to do it and where to go. This is why; instruction is the best builder and means of sustainability of wealth and other aspects of life. We are on a path to receive, sustain, prolong or uphold wealth as far as the earth and the heaven remains.

Whether you are a student, working, retired, engaged, house wife, looking for a job or desiring a new job change, it just doesn't matter; what you are about to learn will not only launch you into wealth but sustain your wealth for at least four generations. This principle is not a respecter of persons or type of work engagements; public servants, private businesses, or individual.

Money and Wealth

Money is not wealth. Money is only a seed for wealth. Wealth is any money that has the capacity to be multiplied and be sustained. Some have money but have not been able to convert it to wealth. Therefore you can run into money by mistake but you consciously create wealth. Wealth comes by specific wealth instructions.

Investment unto wealth is gradual where the various gradual channels can be multiplied and re-multiplied; thereby guaranteeing a multiplied income effect with sustainability.

There are specific financial instructions that guarantee specific financial success. Financial wisdom is the ability to adhere to financial instruction to command, magnet, multiply and sustain finance peacefully anywhere on the surface of the earth. For instance, typhoid fever and cancer are all sicknesses but require some specific drugs to handle each for health recovery; more so someone who is financially broke need a money and wealth instruction to brake off.

How Does Money Answers to all Things?

Yes, money answers to all things but does not mean money solve all problems; if not people would not die. God solves all problems and God cannot be reduced to money. Also, money can only answer all things only if available and used appropriately. One question that must remain in our consciousness is *who is the owner of money*? The Maker of the Universe is the owner. I have heard that when Adolf Hitler, the front-liner of the 1st and 2nd world wars wanted to die; he said all is money must be poured on the ground in front of his house and that he should be buried with an open hand naked. Why? That the world should know that he brought nothing and he is taking nothing back and also that while his doctors watched helplessly and could do nothing. In order words, his money could not save him and not even his world class specialist doctors.

But we need money to get wealthy; achieve what we need to and affect lives positively everywhere by proving God and His principles as true. The knowledge or understanding of the purpose of money will allow and order its effective and efficient use in our lives. Because where purpose is lacking, wastage, abuse and regret is inevitable. Money must be channeled into wealth and must be used to serve God and help people, else it cannot be sustained.

The Multiplier Effect Model

Every money is a seed that needs to be planted, watered and harvested or multiplied. Money is the fasted yielding seed in the world. It is one of God's quickest supernatural demonstrations of miracles.

The three (3) Key Principles to money Seed

1. **The Principle of kind:** Money seed brings money or more money seeds. A seed is a seed no matter how small. Money seed does not need to be huge before it can yield, it only needs to be sown. For instance, $1 is a seed so much as $5, $10, $200 or $1m

2. **The Principle of Growth:** A seed must grow if planted or water correctly. All money can grow but not all money seed is multipliable.

3. **The Principle of Multiplication and Sustainability:** Money seed can be multiplied into wealth. A money seed is capable of multiplying at least 100 of its kind everywhere in the world.

Arriving from the 3 main points above; it means if sown correctly $1 can bring at least $100 or more, and every $5 can yield $500 or $1m for every $1000. This can happen only if we understand how this works and follow up. I believe money seed is the fastest yielding seed in the universe.

Quotes from My Desk

1. *A journey of 1000 miles begins with a vision or plan of the destination while steps follow. Start Now.*

2. *Every job is to help you released your potentials for more success.*

3. *Your vision is your plan as well as your future. Your plan is your attack and defence system.*

4. *Revenge brings poverty to the life of a man. The opposite is God's recompense plan for us. Revenge is an expression of bitterness and unforgiveness. Rejection and disfavour dwells with bitterness.*

5. *The right to know precedes the right to vote and be voted for.*

PART TWO:

Creative Personal, Career and Development with Office Ethics

Chapter One: Introduction Expert Two

There is always a need for qualitative training and retraining of for every endeavour; in personal, business and organisational efficiency. This can be personally or corporately deployed. There is no doubt to saying there is always much to be learnt from experience even as the work goes on, but that is the most hardest part to take because most times it leads to loss and damage of personal and organisation effects. Excellence in duties can be efficiently achieved with a plan and purpose based on training and updated work ethics. This is in the reality that in every location there is a rule for entering and remaining there. What you will learn from this multi-dimensional book will introduce and guide you to adaptation and most successful techniques in life; personal and career wise. Here is a guide for effective management of information, outstanding and noticeable inter-personal skills, and how-best to manage your boss and managerial ways of implementing work standards across board. Also, learn how to develop personal attitude to work because you may not like your job now but you will need to succeed there first because of the future you desire. In this second part; the summary of our dealings is to connote excellence. We believe that Excellency is not a destination, it is a journey. Do you know why? It is because the excellence of yesterday can be the mediocre or the average of today.

Chapter Two: Personal Growth and Development Excellence

Personal growth and development is a daily affair, like bathing. Although bathing is not compulsory everyday but it is necessary in order to avoid stench or stink and for anyone to feel good; that is, it is not 'a do or die affair'. A lot of mad people on the streets of any beautiful city have not had their bathe for a while; say months and they are not dead yet.

So also is personal and growth and development for effectiveness; you may not build yourself now and you may not die as a result but you will really be limiting your progress and self esteem and quietly become a dumping ground. Here, we are talking about ordering your step in time and in shape and succeeding in your life and work place. If you can manage an hour effectively you can manage your day, if you can manage your day; you can manage your life and career. **Hour = Day = Life**.

Eleven (11) keys to Personal Growth and Development

1. **Goals: Daily, Monthly, Quarterly or Yearly.**

    Get a note; simple but good enough that cannot not be easily destroyed. You can also automate wit alarm system your 'to-do-list' using your mobile or similar machines Write down even the smallest assignment and the time to accomplish same. Keep them on sight to keep refreshing your memory and thought to pull the solutions or opportunities closer to you wherever you may be. It helps you to manage time effectively. This is the best way to activate your mental power to see possibilities and opportunities to act.

2. **Time your activities.**

    If you don't value time, you cannot grow. Although time is renewable; that is why the world goes round and round but how renewable your time be is determined by how effective you use your time now to regain lost opportunities. The President of your country and everyone else you know including me and you has 24hrs a day. Our level of accomplishing a task, goal, or plan tests our time management and discipline. Set time for everything for example: meeting with Oketa, Daniel; 10-30am. This is how you will value your time and other people's time. If you don't value my timing, you don't value me. Time is the fuel of my engine; time is the fuel for my brain.

3. **Planning: don't just plan, plan in Detail**

It is one huge thing to have a goal. It is another to plan how to achieve it. When you plan, it shows that you have an expectation. To plan is to have a vision or a future. Planning is a detail of your goals. Taking out time to plan (30-1hr) purposefully for the next day or for anything else gives you an edge over others or circumstances. You can use some part of the night to plan. Always expand your goals with planning.

4. **Do important things first**

We have values and high values. Provide solutions to high value targets first and others will easily be solved. This has to do with priority. To be honest with you, there is priority in everything and this can only be measured in your plan. For instance buying a car must not be as important as getting the money to buy the car first. In other words you can't start going to buy a car without first having the money. Remember high value things bring more success or high value results. Set your priority right even with a plan.

5. **Take proper care of your body.**

   You can only plan and achieve your plans, manage time when you are in health. Take time to walk or exercise; eat as good and much as fits you; and do not over feed your system; it causes laziness and sluggishness. Do not purposeful violate health principles or put yourself in a fix and then begin to ask God for a miracle. And if you are having a health challenge already, I will ask you to work it out by taking appropriate medication and believe even with God you are healed.

6. Learning and Growth

Do not wait for your employer to train you anytime. In fact all employers like those who on their own can bring innovative ideas and solutions for profit. Train or build yourself by reading books in the direction of need. Make purposeful research, by reading and studying a lifestyle; not just newspaper or gossips magazines. The books you can buy show your level of value for knowledge and insight. You should be able to buy books than you can buy clothes. One single idea or information from a book can give you 100 hundreds of cloths. One day I came home with books as usually and my brother said; *you will just be buying books-what for?* But not to my surprise, I saw him glancing through that particular book and I am sure he got something from there even if he did not tell me. What does not mean? Proximity to anything determines accessibility. If you have books, you will look at them regularly or once in a while and then make it a habit. Make a decree to read, buy or borrow at least one book a month. Make a particular time a reading or planning time. Hear this, most secret of great men that you can tap from are hidden in their books. Most times they hardly had the time or opportunity to say it all or in detail by spoken words.

7. **Build your Relationship**

Life is Relationship; business is relationship; family is relationship; career is relationship. Everyone around you is important and they are your relatives by association, location or choice. The best way to build relationship is not to easily be offended with or by people. Be patience with people and their level of understanding or knowledge. If everybody or everything can just offend or annoy you quickly, then you are cheap.

8. **Take the Opportunity of where you are now**

You may not be where you want to be now; most people in fact everyone is not because life should be progressive until we die. And anywhere you are now is a step to where you are heading. And you may not be where you really desire now but anywhere you are has its own advantage and contribution for your future. Use it wisely. If you realize this, you will live a *more positive* life. Living positively helps you to identify opportunities easily. You know, the word *more* is used with *positive* above to mean that you need to go extra mile to live positively; because there are always negative news and things competing for your attention. Make sure you put only things that inspire you in from of you.

9. Do not Complain; do something

If you complain about people, circumstances etc, you damage your godly self esteem. Perpetual complaining is a disease that eats ups good habits, worsens the situation, discourages others, and hides opportunities. Complaining is 90% expressed by speech in numerous words, anger and expression or display of un-satisfaction by expecting too much from people. Always say something like *"we need this or that" "we should do this or that" rather than "this is bad" or "things are not working" etc.*

10. **Be a Helper Always**

A helper is a solution provider. No matter who you are, you are where you are because you are meant to solve a problem. Problem is the seed for money. When you solve a problem, you create a divine debt for a reward. See yourself as a helper so you can value and reward the help of others to also facilitates your reward. Cease to be only on the receiving side in anything or area of your life. The amount of problems you can solve determines the amount of reward you will receive.

11. **Personal Relationship with God.**

If you are not getting enough understanding of God how and where you are, then you will need to change. You cannot be really personally successful without a personal relationship with your God. You see, there is a difference between the use of the phrases ' My God' *and* 'Our God'. There are specific instructions you will need from God for your personal success.

Chapter Three: Becoming Boss-Wise: How to Manage Your Boss

Who is your boss? Anyone who gives you instructions and/or determines your reward is your boss. Boss are not picked, they pick others that would be loyal to them but committed to their duties. But in case you had the opportunity of picking your boss, such opportunity is an uncommon one and it puts you into a position to live-out your expectation to gain more trust and value. An incompetent manager or boss can make your life depressed and miserable and vice verse. They need your assistance and you need their assistance to succeed. The more effective your manager gets, the more pleasant your days and work are likely to be. All bosses must seek to be a role model to their subordinates by their efficiency.

Eight (8) Ways for Effective Boss Management

1. **Be ready and determined to be successful by making your boss successful:** If your boss succeeds, you succeed together and vice verse.

This will have to make you pray for them even in your secret.

2. **Accept that your boss has the power to direct your activities and give you instructions:** He or she is your instructor; no matter how brave you might be. Accept the fact and provide the needed support. He takes the glory or the disgrace.

3. **Be Excellent:** Don't expect your boss to be a perfect but you work towards you own excellence. Managers are people who have short comings also. Recognize your boss weak point, add strength and manage them effectively by providing the needed support.

4. **Study your boss and what brings him/her happiness:**

   Ask him questions if you have to. Asking questions is the best way to learn faster. You do not only put the responder in a position to operate on what they agree or disagree with, but this will help you to work smarter by what you know or expect.

5. **Let your boss trust your ability and credibility:** Produce quality results, meet deadlines, and stay within your budget. When you identify a problem, make sure you seek to provide the solution. Contribute new ideas and suggestions. Share useful information with your boss.

6. **Compliment your boss as at when due:** Managers hear lots of complaints, but few employees or subordinates ever bother to give their boss a kind word of complement. Kind word of complement can heal and encourage work place progress.

7. **No Private affair:** Private affair weakens both you and your boss's firmness and even objectivity in times of need. Remember the more he succeeds, so also you do. Your first goal is to succeed yourself by being upright in your decisions and character.

Chapter Four: How to build Effective Communication and Interpersonal Skills

What is Effective Communication?

Communication is an order of channel between one or two persons or groups. It is a means of taking and giving. That is, an effective communication requires a response (verbally and none-verbally) during and after an instruction or direction. Communication can be very effective when there is an agreement or understanding and the intended result is achieved from an instruction given or received.

What are Interpersonal Skills?

Interpersonal skill is one's ability to communicate effective and interact with other people, both individually and in groups effectively and result-full especially in fulfillment of a goal. Developing strong interpersonal skills brings success in both professional and personal live. Organizations seek to hire staff with 'strong interpersonal skills' because they need those who will work well in a team and are able to communicate effectively with colleagues, customers and clients. People with good interpersonal skills are usually perceived as optimistic; (positive), calm; (gentle), confident (well informed) and Charismatic (admirable).

What Interpersonal Skill is Not

- Your ability to shout or argue your point out is not a good interpersonal skill.

- Your ability or desire to keep talking or tell stories even with colleagues often is not one also.

- And again, it is not your ability to talk to everyone or stranger effectively without a beneficial end or expectation.

Practicing Interpersonal Skill

Anything that is practiced becomes easy. Practice makes or brings perfection. Routine provides a great edge. I am talking of a life style of magnet that transcend above cultural, religious, political and economic barriers for success in all life endeavour with a spiritual improvement. Application of interpersonal skills should not be taken for granted anywhere. If life is a network of relationships; then we all need to practice these skills to manage and profit from our relationships all round. That is why I prefer to call interpersonal skills as life skills. Perfect Interpersonal skill gives life and hope to the practitioner and others.

Seven (7) Best ways to Practice Interpersonal Skills

1. **Be a good Listener:** Always listen and don't be in a hurry to talk. This can allow you catch up with people both verbally and non-verbally.

2. **Be Slow and choose your words:** Because your words matters and can affect people and things positively or negatively, you should be very careful with your words. Select them by thinking about the effect first. Practice clarity and learn to seek feedback nicely to ensure your message has been understood.

3. **Ask questions:** Encourage others to engage in communication by asking appropriate questions

to develop your understanding. Those who ask questions tend to always be on the listening side. Try as much as possible to show real concern or interest in the people you talk to. Ask questions and seek clarification on any points that could be easily misunderstood. Do not claim to know everything at a time and say you don't know if you don't.

4. **Be Positive:** Try to remain positive and cheerful else you drive people and good away. Don't always think that everyone has a bad agenda at first sight. This does not mean you should trust every one especially that you have not trusted before. People are much more likely to be drawn to you if you can maintain a positive attitude.

5. **Empathise:** Fix yourself in people's position by imagining yourself in their shoes if you were to be involved. We all have one or two privileges that others don't to know or have something. This will help you understand their needs with appropriate response.

6. **Don't be Nervous:** When you are nervous; it is either you are hiding something, or being afraid of the now or future. If this become the case, result to a quiet moment and check. Do not transfer problems of one place to another. You are nervous, your confidence drops with your ability to communicate clearly. If your confidence drops quickly, take a time out or close the meeting or conservation to gather more information if you can. It is what you know that gives you confidence.

Chapter Five: Effective Managerial Techniques and Channels

A person who holds a management position in an organization is required to think strategically and conceptually in order to achieve organizational goals. Management involves far more than just telling others what to do. Managers or management must represent by doing what they say in order to lead or enforce their plans. This makes a management tasking and manifold as well as rewarding. In other to teach others or subordinates, they must be the think tank and also a doer of their ideas. This lesson will describe

1. Core The General Four functions of management,

2. Determining Work Ethic and Standards and

3. Office Automation, Information and Visitor Management

1. The Four General Core Functions of Management

These four managerial functions of Planning, Organizing, Leading and Controlling has become the generally accepted division of functions of management. These Include:

1. **Planning**: this is goal setting and detailing or idea generation. This makes planning one of the biggest time consuming of any good manager. All the following depends greatly on the plan on ground.

2. **Organizing**: This involves appointing both human and other resources that are needed for a goal. Organizing also involves apportioning rewards for outstanding efforts.

3. **Leading:** The best way to lead is to do first such as to lead by example. Leading rely more on accomplished goals or achieved goals by an excellent personnel.

4. **Controlling;** This involves delegation of duties, management of output until the desired plan, goal or target is achieved.

2. Determining Work Ethic and Standards

Work ethics and standards are an organization's expectations of acceptable behavior for every member; employer/employees; executives, managers and subordinates. Ethics and standards are the principles that when followed, should produce and promote success and values such as trust, good behavior, fairness, and/or kindness. There is not one regular set of ethics and standards that all organizations follow, but as required by each according and in order to realize her goals and mission. These involve some *the does* and the *don'ts*. I will agree with Dr Mike Mrduck that, *"every environment requires a rule for entering and remaining there"*. Such that you must identify the expectation of your environment in order to adapt for result oriented run.

How to Design Effective Work ethics and Standards

1. **Successful Approaches**: Replicate successful approaches from other organizations by applying generally acceptable principles.

2. **Consider peculiarity:** that is, enforce peculiar ethic as situation or location demands to produce acceptable behaviour and success.

3. **Firmness in Flexibility:** rules change according to the goals and missions. Therefore it is advisable that intents or motives are checked as it relates to applying consequences to non-compliance. Ethics and standard must apply to all under the same condition, location and otherwise.

4. **Focus on the Results:** ethics and standards are not created or designed to target offences or offenders but to advance success. There must a focus most on how successful some ethics have worked or not. This will create positive attitude towards maintaining high standards for work ethics and creates a productive environment in

which people take pride in their work, customers and partners.

Some Internationally Accepted Ethics and Standards

1. **Respect and Communication:** There is a general ethical demand that all employees value each other's opinions, treat customers with dignity and recognize cultural diversity, and show respect in the workplace. This can be achieved or enforced by encouraging strong interpersonal skills and positive attitude.

2. **Cooperation and Teamwork:** Another accepted ethics is the spirit of team-ship in all organization. Cooperation and team is an effective collaboration technique to pool resources, energy to accomplish a collective goal. This can be strengthened by involving subordinates in decision-making meetings and paring and creating teams for a common goal. Make one persons success a challenge but beneficial to all involved.

3. **Appearance and Character:** In many organizations, there are dress codes and great value for good character exhibition or positive attitude to work. This promotes a positive image to others and the outside world. Immoral and unethical performance or behaviour causes distraction, kill productivity and create a bad image for the entire organization.

4. **Attendance and Time Management:** Time management is an appropriate ethic and standard for any organization to succeed meaningfully. The amount of time utilized determines greatly, cost and productively or effectiveness of a thing. Effective time management must be encourage and operated by executives, managers for exemplary transfer to subordinates. This is not only limited to accomplishing a particular task on schedule but arriving for duty, closure and meeting as agreed.

5. **Channeling General Issues:** It is best and effective to have a unit that handles discipline, ethical and

standard matters. This is in order to constantly review, handle issues or complains from employers, employees and the general public.

3. Office Automation, Information and Visitor Management

Office automation is the deployment of diverse ICT, computer machinery and software used to electronically create, collect, store, control, and transfer office information needed for accomplishing basic tasks. Automation creates faster means of executing deals and information transfer and speed up existing procedures. A perfect example of office automation is e-commerce directory; all sales and information are conducted electronically, the use of Local Area Network (LAN) to transmit data, mail with or voice across the network.

The following are listed as some of the advantages of Office Automation

1. Fastness and volume is achieved

2. Smaller staff size is possible.

3. Multiple users at a time.

4. Task reduction for higher productivity

Information Management

Information management (IM) is the collection and direction of information. That is the effective channel of information from one or more sources and the distribution of that information to one or more audience. A better documentation of information helps for quality research and decision making. Information can be electronic or manually or both. This includes data; paper documents, electronic documents, audio, video, etc. A good information management must ensure the transmission of data or instruction from the point of collection to the appropriate user on demand. Electronic transfer of information can be through many paths; LAN, fax, cell phones and web interfaces over the internet.

Information Guiding Principles

According to the Association for Information and Image Management; (AIIM), Information management requires the adoption and adherence to guiding principles that include the following:

1. **Information assets are corporate assets.** This principle should be acknowledged or agreed upon across the organization for effectiveness otherwise any business support for information management.

2. **Information must be made available and shared**. Of course not all information is open to anyone, but in principle the sharing of information acknowledged or fosters the realization of corporate goals.

3. **The needed information of an organization needs to be managed appropriately**. In other words, there should be an effort and guide to save and retrieve information.

Responsibility of Information Management

Information management is a corporate responsibility that needs to be addressed and followed from the upper most senior levels of management to the front line worker. In other words, organizations must be responsible to train her workforce and provide necessary equipments to manage information effectively for successful policy formulation, compliance and assessment.

Visitor Management:

Visitor management involves directing, accessing and informing people within and outside the organization. Visitors are the major component of any organization. Without different nature of visitors and their responses, level of service and product self-assurance may hardly be assessed effectively. Whether an organization is the most profiting in any industry or country, effective visitor management must not be underrated. Visitors can become our most consistent customers and we can make our customers our best sales lead.

Keys to Visitor Management

1. Managing visitors communicates efficiency and protects the organizational image, disposition and content.

2. Visitor management is an essential role in defending sustainability, providing funding and business opportunities.

3. This also is involves the information gathering of visitors profile, their needs, the satisfaction level and other vital information.

Who is a Visitor?

A visitor is anyone who visits an organization for any intention whatsoever. This may be by physically location, or electronically through website or other online medium. For example, anyone who meets a staff of an organization outside the work place but desires any information is also a visitor. Here we have identified three level or types of visitors; physical-office location visitors, electronic visitors and mobile visitors. No one of this must be undervalued, underestimated or failed to be appreciated.

Evaluation and Assessment of Visitors

A good information system of any organization should be able to manage visitors. Evaluation and assessment can be done with satisfaction enquiry; opinions and suggestions. This can be manually or electronically. Electronically, the use of internet, computer, Video tools; CCTV, software etc is applicable, while manually, may be direct contact or other otherwise with manual records . Visitor management can be evaluated and appraised periodically to check if a promotional or marketing strategy is effective. In the world of diverse economic and social and spiritually motivated reasons and security verification, visitor information can be very important.

Chapter Six: How to Build a Positive Attitude to Work

Key points

1. Positive attitude to work or live is not an option; it is a must for survival.
2. You are either positive or you are negative; there is no middle ground.
3. Positive and negative is an expression of inner strength. Your strength can be positive or negative.
4. Your inner strength determines your visible strength. It is first expressed by your thoughts; this is why your thoughts can affect you mentally and physical actions.
5. To succeed and register success on others; you must be too positive to be negative.
6. Positive or negative attitude is built and it is not an accident. It is not a gift but a decision. It is the buildup of what you hear or see and think about which is sooner or later expressed

Ten (10) Steps to building Positive Attitude

1. **Comparison:** Comparison is a positive tool for progress only if used correctly. Compare yourself only with your last result and not with others. This does not mean you should not admire and

compliment the good in others. The key is to out-do yourself yesterday in your today.

2. **Nothing is impossible:** Noting is impossible but impossibilities are only achieved or clarified by planning not by accident. Accidents are negative uncontrolled happenings. You can be the next person on the newspaper headline across the globe tomorrow morning; it is possible.

3. **Value or recognize others.** Recognize greatness in others and honour them for their difference. Honoring is more of gift of substances and not speech. This is also the path of honour for those who have supported you. Relate more with those who inspire you knowingly or unknowingly. Ask them necessary questions of their progress. Run away from negative people

4. **Be patient:** If you are to be patience; it is because you know something that others don't know. It is because you have a promise, a vision or a plan with which you are expectant of a better result. For instance, there is nothing wrong if your first

answer will always be "let me think about this". *Patience is expressed deeply by your behavior while you wait for an outcome not only the amount of time spent.*

5. **Do not offend others by the extent of your positivity:** if those around you are positive and happy as you are, you will succeed more. Therefore your positively should not leave others in bad shape, offended or negative. If you value others and are patient, you would not try to multiply their negativity. For example, if you are playing music in your office which is shared by someone who is not in that mode and he or she requests you to turn it off or reduce it; please do or manage the volume carefully. It shows that you are matured and have empathy.

6. **Be Open minded:** Those who seek to be well informed and deliberately work towards it are opened minded. That is, they don't wait for others to do it for them; they do it by themselves consciously. To be opened minded does not mean

to allow all things into access into your system; but to seek the right Knowledge or information carefully by hearing, eyeing, permitting. If you can choose food then you can choose other contents for your benefit. Your thought is highly dependent of what you take it. Avoid negative books, news, report or people. But, it is not enough to avoid them; put the good book, news, report or people close to you and access them always. For instance, something that does not add to your joy, subtract your joy.

7. **Communicate needs.** Statement carry weight and even more weight by the way there are spoken or communicated. You must be polite in your questions, actions and request. To make a request is far better than to complain. If someone makes you feel negative, like a friend, tell then in a nice way how you feel much preferably later if need be. Be very careful with what you say, you are helped, trapped or release by your speech.

8. **Be creative;** if you are creative, you will always seek positive solutions to things and from things you could not control. Being creative help you to help others solve their problems. Always seek an advantage over all situations to enforce your creativity in solutions. Creativity always comes out of what seems like chaos, formlessness or problematic.

9. **Appearance.** You clothing tells about you before you arrive. Your appearance and dressing speaks when you don't speak or before you speak. Your dressing can leave others offensive, think negative or positively and lively. What is fashionable or trendy may not be what fits you. Clothing is a makeup; and you choose your makeup for success. Your make-up determines the type of attention you attract. If your dress is offensive (expensive or not), it means it does not fit you, and do not communicate a good image or nor fit the use.

10. **Association:** Your association determines by far how successful you can be or grow anywhere in

life. Avoid anyone who is not going your way in life. Leave those who are not willing to follow your path of goodness and success.

Chapter Seven: Maximizing Your Opportunities and Exploit

You need to succeed and succeed well. You need to succeed and transfer your succeed to someone else. You need to succeed; and begin to succeed from where you are. The understanding of the following five points can greatly influence our success and establish them.

1. The One Secret of Wealth and Business Building
2. The Power of Collaboration
3. Power Yourself Online
4. The God Factor
5. Mentorship Wisdom

1. The One Secret of Wealth and Business Building

Start, Just Start or Begin: The force or push to start is very important and is one of the greatest secret for the success of anything in business or life. Everything started and started small compared to the progress they may have made. Once there is a vision or plan, a step must be taken for a mark. Start something believe in, or plan for no matter how small or big your action might seem because those help needed for the continuation must come. You are more exposed to help and more prone get it once a thing is started because starting small is creativity in action. Everyone like and welcome creativity. 90% those doing big businesses did not start as big as they are today. In business, for instance if you say you want to start asking people, banks or government for loans and grants; you may wait a long time and may get very discouraged. But once you start something and it's moving, help will locate you, more opportunities will be realized and better way of doing things will show up. At that time, you may not need to answer many business terms and jargons because you are in search of help; your business presences, opportunities and successes speak. The world did not start with anybody giving the next person a loan, but those who offered what they had and got what they needed. It was moneyless, but money came out from nowhere. Those who have something, more will be added. Think creatively and start creatively, just start.

2. The Power of Collaboration

The Fold Concept: A fold is something that is over or round about each other; that binds or holds together. I want to use this as an example of partnership to illustrative its multimillion dollar, diverse and massive dimensional successful effect in business relationship or venture.

In as much as there is a powerful successful effect of fold so also is a powerful negative effect of fold in any relationship or arrangement. This is why your association must be right. For the association to be right the expectations must be spelt out. For the expectation to be assimilated, adaptation is inevitable.

Dr. Mike Murdock would say it this way; "every environment I enter has its expectation; I must I identify the expectation and must be willing to adapt to achieve my expectation". If you cannot adapt, you cannot release your potentials. The release of your potentials will help to fulfill every expectation. When we are one (1), we are good; when we are two- we are better off, when we are three and above, we are at the Best.

3. Power Yourself Online

"Nothing happens by accident in the world of computers, the Net, and customer response. There is always a reason for what happens; good or bad, and that reason is you"
Ken Envoy

You should build an online presence as a business or person. Don't underestimate the need to get online as little or much as you can. Use blog or possibly website to create an only presence and continue therein. If you are the one that uses the internet for sending and receiving emails, reading newspapers, and sharing pictures and updates on facebook and other social networks alone...then your time of change has come for the better. There is still much to be gained and explored through the internet. Let's consider the internet table usage table below:-

Worldwide Internet users

	2005	2010	2013
World population	6.5 billion	6.9 billion	7.1 billion
Not using the Internet	84%	70%	61%
Using the Internet	16%	30%	39%
Users in the developing world	8%	21%	31%

Users in the developed world	51%	67%	77%
			Estimate.
Source: International Telecommunications Union, 2014.			

If as at 2013, 61% of the world is yet to come to use the internet, we still have much to take care of as they come in daily. This confirms that the internet is yet full of profit, money and income and it is just the beginning. The internet is the fastest and the largest market in the world and is still expanding. It is accessible anytime or day. The internet gives everyone huge opportunities to reach millions of people at every point in time as the world total internet users estimate (2013) stands at about 2billion (i.e **2,730,000.000**). This is expected to grow to over 50% by 2020 as the world internet and computer penetration increase daily.

For instance, in 1994 only 3% of American classrooms had access to the Internet but by 2002, 92% did. So also will it be in our countries and continents in the near future. *What are you lunching now through the internet in preparation for the future?*

Imagine if you can reach some additional or constant 50 successful customers monthly requiring your product or service online. With the internet, whatever you have or know can be transferred or exchanged. It has been established that the internet right now is the largest advertisement medium in the entire world and it will remain so even in the next 100 years. For example in 2013, Internet users in China alone represent 25% of the world's total Internet users because of their huge population, also online education are increasing everyday and becoming more effective around the world.

4. The God Factor

There is no middle ground in Divinity, because God is never in a double standard mode; if you are not on this side, then you are on the other side. That is to say, if you are not using your human effort with God's blessing, then you are using your human effort alone. He later is dangerous because results cannot be sustained even if achieved. There is no body on the surface of the earth that does not need God's favour and miracle, just not one. Your complete reliance and seeking to know God will determine how far good you can always go or become or successful. If you continue to be on the ungodly side, you will ways be on the tiny side. Connect to a Higher Spiritual Authority where you are with a yearning and deliberate actions to know Him more. If you believe God authored your life, then He has an authority to know better. The idea is to seek to understand your God daily; He will tell you and show you more successful ways to live because no one would want to leave his children empty handed or ineffective.

5. Mentorship Wisdom

Mentorship is someone you choose to follow and honour in order to learn from their mistake and fast track your own success. Clearly and most at times they must have gone ahead of us mostly in the same road that we seek to follow. By natural and my experience, they know better. Divinity works well in mentorship; because, you ability to respect and honour someone who is clearly ahead that you can see facilities your desire to love and honour God that you are unable to see. Find a mentor, reach out them and let them know your want to follow their steps to succeed. Get more of them by their books, tapes and other materials to learn their success stories. Your mentor can be a good support and elevation. If you show me whom you summit to and I will show you what will submit to you. If you show me whom you partner and I will show you what will partner with you. If you show me your company and I will show you what will accompany you. If you show me who you are disposed to and I will show you what will be disposed to you.

Quotes

Dr Pastor Paul Enenche and Others

- Right Impact might-

In other words, what you know that belongs to you determines how audacious and powerful you can be.

- Persistence is the cure for resistance as excellence is the cure to every prejudice or discrimination.

- Association determines assimilation and acceleration-

- Man is not designed to say what he has but have what he says-Dr Paul Enenche- *The Law of Words.*

- It takes the lion heart to take the lion share-Bishop David Oyedepo.

- An angry man is a stupid man always-Chenu Achebe

From My Desk:

6. *Providing solution answers problems. A problem is a means of learning how to fight and win as a means of promotion.*

7. *As far as the heavens and earth remains, answers and solutions to challenging national problems or difficulties dwells with the sons of God.*

8. *A 10 years evil plan can be truncated by just a tiny revelation, because once a plan begins, the revelation begins to cook in another camp.*

9. *Every man is designed to use what has, because every man has something.*

www.ingramcontent.com/pod-product-compliance
Lightning Source LLC
Chambersburg PA
CBHW021405170526
45164CB00002B/510